COMMUNION
OF SAINTS

George A. Maloney, S.J.

LIVING FLAME PRESS

325 RABRO DRIVE, HAUPPAUGE, N.Y. 11788

Edited By Emilie Teutschman

Cover: *In His Image*
By William Zdinak

Cover Art Available Through
IHI
P.O. Box 263
Wayne, PA 19087

First Printing 1988

Imprimi Potest: Patrick J. Burns, S.J., Provincial, Wisconsin
Province of the Society of Jesus, May 20, 1987

ISBN: 0-914544-73-X

Published by:
Living Flame Press/325 Rabro Drive/Hauppauge, N.Y. 11788

Printed at Mark IV Press, Hauppauge, N.Y.

Copyright©1988 George A. Maloney, S.J.
Printed in the United States of America

Dedication

To Sister Miriam Murphy

A pioneer in ecumenism before it was popular. One who understands communion of saints and suggested that I write this book.

Acknowledgements

Deepest gratitude to Patricia Metta and Mary Louise Leonard for their excellent typing of my manuscript, and to Sister Joseph Agnes of the Sisters of Charity of Halifax and to June Culver, my secretary of CONTEMPLATIVE MINISTRIES, for proofreading the manuscript and for their many suggestions.

TABLE OF CONTENTS

INTRODUCTION

The effectiveness of a true religion lies in its ability to bring into a unity of love God and His creation. One approach is to present God as extrinsic to His creatures, especially human beings. The worlds of the infinite and the finite are separated in such a view. The world of matter is dichotomized from the world of the spirit.

God, in such a view, is presented as the Supreme Being, independent of His creatures, perfect and unchangeable. He is static with no emotions and no interpersonal relationships with His imperfect creatures, except that of a fearful, vindictive, punishing God. He rules His universe by immutable laws on the physical, psychological and spiritual levels.

We human beings, in such a view, are presented as material beings, living in an objective world and dominated in our relationships with God, other human beings and the entire cosmos by impersonal relationships of an *I-It*. Through science, we in the Western world have replaced God as the center of all reality and substituted ourselves. We are scientific observers, looking with detachment at an objective world (and God Himself) that one can control by the human mind.

We look at God and other persons or material objects and we think we are a separated subject, "objectively" viewing a static world of concrete, self-existent objects, all independent of each other. We pray to God as to another objective person, usually to receive a favor. He is "above" us, outside of us.

In such a religious view, we human beings see and, yet, we do not see. We see beautiful flowers and fail to see the beautiful face of God shining through the flowers. We see men and women, as the blind man of Bethsaida confessed, as "trees walking" (Mk 8:24). So much of God's loving presence walks into our lives each day, at each moment, but we fail to see Him, especially in each other. We are "invaded" constantly by God's energizing love in each event. Yet, most of us are asleep to that presence.

A Second View

The other religious approach breaks through the heavy separation of the world of matter from the spiritual world. In this view, God is always immanently present inside of His creation. Any separation is an illusion called "sin." Diligent asceticism and purification of the inner eye will eventually effect an enlightenment to reveal what always was the only *real*. We are a part of God in our truest selves. God is we and we are the Absolute!

In such an approach, there is no separation from the material world. There is death only to the illusions that keep us from the truth of our oneness with the Divine Absolute. Any sense of a unique, separated self-hood divides and leads to ignorance of the basic reality: God is all! All is God!

A Third Approach

There is still a third approach. That is what Christianity alone brings to the world religions. The power of Christianity lies in its ability through its teachings but, more so, through the active presence of God encountered in sacraments, in individual prayer and in a community of love that exalts the uniqueness of each member. This is discovered in the loving unity of the members transformed into participators of the divine triune community who live for the happiness of others.

Christianity begins with a dualism. God is the Creator. The limited beings of angelic spirits, human creatures and all the rest of material creation are never God and will always remain *other* than God. In His divine essence, God does not need His creatures to add to His perfection. He is self-sufficient, perfect, never to be coerced by any outside force. Before God there is *no-thing*!

Yet, Christianity presents us with a seeming paradox. This Divine Being is One. There is no other. Yet, this God has freely consented to create creatures and our entire universe. He has revealed to His rational creatures, angels and human beings, the awesome mystery that is beyond our human, rational understanding.

God is not merely one. God is also many. God is a one-community, a union of loving persons. These persons are three. They discover their uniqueness through their differentiating relations to each other, but always in the same Spirit of the person of Love.

Christianity believes in a historical person, born of a mother, Mary, in Palestine, known as Jesus of Nazareth. He came among men and taught, healed the sick, performed miracles, died as a public criminal because He claimed He was one with God and then His followers believed He rose from the dead. He poured out His Spirit, Who enabled His followers to live in the mystery that He is of the same nature as His Heavenly Father.

God — A Community of Loving Persons

For those who believe *in* Jesus Christ, God is revealed as a community of loving persons. Father and Son ecstatically love each other in the binding, personalized Love, the Holy Spirit. The *I* is the child of the *We*. Within the Trinity there is a oneness through love. Yet, the very love, which is the Holy Spirit, brings about the unique personhood of each person. Utter freedom is measured by the all-consuming desire to give one's being away for the happiness of the other. Freedom and love in God are inseparable.

Out of such circular movement of love that unites as it differentiates, God, as one and three, one and many, explodes outward to "other" their loving community in creation. Love needs to expand, to be shared and, thus, it becomes incarnated through enfleshment. Such love, incarnated in creatures, paradoxically can never be separated as subject toward an objective world.

God is! God is also Creator. There is only God. Yet God and His creatures are in intimate oneness, yet not identical. God is within His creation. Yet God is always "beyond" His creatures. God is immaterial, yet the mystery of His love teaches us that God also has materialized Himself in His creation of Love. God is always beyond, transcendent of His World. Yet God is immanently present inside His material creation by His uncreated energies of love.

God, triune community of one and many, perfect and unchangeable, has freely chosen to share His community of one and many loving, divine persons with others, created by

4

Him according to His own image and likeness (Gn 1:26). God so loves this created world in which He works with His un-created energies of love in each atom and sub-atomic particle throughout the created universe.

Jesus Christ—The Bridge-Builder

All such inner presence of uncreated, loving energies reach a peak of concentrated, microcosmic presence in God's only begotten Son incarnate. "Yes, God loved the world so much that he gave his only Son, so that everyone who believes in him may not be lost, but may have eternal life" (Jn 3:16). Now God is love personalized in humanity. God gives us the great *Way*, the great Bridge-Builder, Jesus Christ, Who spans the infinite and the finite, God and His creatures, eternity and time, Spirit and matter.

God's plan from all eternity is moving by a personalized Center, Who directs, from within material creation, all crea-tures toward a goal that is the very same Center, the Trinity of one and many. God's immanent, triune community of Father, Son and Holy Spirit is becoming "othered" in matter by God's "two hands—Jesus Christ and His Holy Spirit," as St. Irenaeus of the 2nd century expressed the mys-tery of infinity touching finity.

This Divine Word made flesh died to image the perfect love of God the Father through His Spirit for each of us. The Father raised Him in glory from the dead. Now the risen Savior lives within the individual Christ and in the corporate Body of Christ, the Church, empowering the other actual or potential members of Christ's Body by love to aid the Spirit to bring them into a greater union with Christ, their Head. We are called and actually are made "participators" in God's very own nature, sharers in the trinitarian life (2 P 1:4).

5

The Communion of Saints

This book has been written to invite you, reader, to ponder prayerfully God's eternal plan in which He wishes to share with all His creatures the triune love as manifested in Christ Jesus and His Spirit. I have taken the ancient term: "communion of saints," as expressed in the Apostles' Creed, and have sought to search into what this *communion* should mean in terms of our personal relationships with God-Trinity, with Jesus Christ, Head of His Body, the Church, with each other and with the entire created world.

Moving always in the dynamic dialect of loving relationships between ourselves on this earth and Christ, our *Way* to the fulfillment, the *pleroma* of God's eternal plan, I explore the spirit-world. Can we lovingly relate in union and distinction with our departed loved ones? Can we communicate with them and help them by our prayers? Can the saints in glory help us on earth?

We examine the specific relationships which we and the saints can have toward the departed who struggle in therapy to bring Christ into all their past experiences that were closed to his divinizing presence through self-centeredness. This state of therapy we continue to call by the traditional term of *purgatory*, but we seek to examine such teaching in terms of personal relationships within the one Body of Christ.

The doctrine about and existence of angelic spirits, both good and bad, have been rejected by many modern persons as very "unscientific." We examine this topic as a God-given presence of His loving, protective power. We try to see how angels are God's gifts to us and to see our relationship with them.

Mary, the Intercessor

I single out Mary, the chosen Mother of God, as a concrete expression of how we can be in communication with the order of saints in glory. We see how the fundamental principle of God's salvific order, a reflection of the 'pass-over' experience within the Trinity, applies to Mary and all of us. The closer we are united in the Body with Christ, our Head, the more we seek to forget ourselves and surrender to let God's Word and His Spirit drive us forth in loving service to help others in need.

We, still living on this earth and forming the Church Militant, cannot be separated from, and unconcerned with, the needs of other fellow-pilgrims, as well as the departed in purgatory and the saints in glory. Christ calls us to share in His high-priestly intercession, but only to the degree that our prayers of intercession are enfleshed by oblational love, whereby we share in Christ's sacrifice as we lovingly serve the departed.

This leads us to the awesome mystery of the Eucharist, the peak of the sacramental life of the Church and the goal of God's creation of all creatures in His Word. We receive God's gift of Jesus Christ in His sacrifice and sacrament of love. We commemorate Christ's sacrifice of love for other members of Christ's Body. We live the Eucharist as the offering of our prayers for others becomes also an emptying love in service for all members of Christ's Body.

We conclude this book by presenting heaven as a loving process of continued growth, that begins now as we live death-resurrection through the power of Christ risen and His Holy Spirit. We see Heaven as interpersonal relationships that are always growing between ourselves and the Trinity and between ourselves and all other creatures created by God in His Word and brought to fulfillment by Jesus Christ with the cooperation of the living members of His Body, the angelic spirits and all human beings, who continually surrender to God in His Word to build by loving service Christ's Body. Trinity is more Trinity as the total Christ reflects that inner community of love of an *I-Thou-We* family of God and His children.

Conclusion

Thus, the doctrine of the communion of saints is a powerful summary of the plan of God Who wishes to share His divine, triune life with His creatures. He does this through us transformed, healthy members of the Body of Christ, as we extend God's life to others. But only to the degree that Christ's love within us allows us to be so one with Him will each of us understand our privilege that has always been God's: "A man can have no greater love than to lay down his life for his friends" (Jn 15:13).

I add an appendix on *spiritism* and devil possession to warn against a false communion with the spirit world. This does not build up the Body of Christ, but tends to create more darkness and self-centeredness to war against the Kingdom of God.

I pray that the insights presented in this book may be received by you, the reader, in a prayerful, reflective manner. True communion of saints cannot be taught solely through rational concepts. It is rooted in the mystery of God's infinite, humble love for us and all His creation. It deals with interpersonal relationships between each of us toward God, toward Christ and His Spirit, toward each other, those living on this earth, those departed and, yet, not totally integrated into Christ, and those in glory. It is all about the uniqueness of each creature and the exciting process of becoming children of God which will know no end as we learn to live for Christ. May we learn what St. Paul learned by insight in his earthly life and which he is still learning by loving service toward the members of Christ: "There is only Christ: he is everything and he is in everything" (Col 3:11).

Midway City, CA   George A. Maloney, S.J.
Feast of the Exaltation of the Cross

Chapter One

WE FORM ONE BODY

Of all the doctrinal statements found in the Church's earliest creeds, especially in the Apostles' Creed, the one stating our belief in the communion of saints is the one least understood among Christians and, therefore, the one that has least importance for practical Christian living.

What does this statement mean to you whenever you recite the Apostles' Creed: "I believe in the .communion of saints"? Does it mean for you only a general belief that saints in glory are in "communion" with us pilgrims on earth and can exercise a power of intercession on our behalf and that of our departed loved ones "suffering in purgatory"?

All this may be true and a part of the traditional belief in our Catholic faith. But there is so much more packed into this short phrase: "communion of saints." Today we live in an age of personalism. We desperately want to become our unique "person." We want so much to know who we really are beyond the role playing and the masks we wear to cover up our hidden true self. This true self lies potentially deep down within ourselves, as a seed in darkness, but has not yet experienced the cracking and splitting apart in order to bring forth new and abundant fruit.

We need, first, to ponder prayerfully in God's spirit of love the great plan of God from all eternity, if we are to understand the riches in the doctrine of the communion of saints.

God is Love

The most fundamental teaching in God's revelation is that God is love (1 Jn 4:8). Jesus, God's image of love enfleshed in human form for our salvation, is the revelation in His person of how great a love God—Father, Son and Holy Spirit—has for each of us. He reveals that His love comes out of the community of love, the Trinity. God is love, not first toward us but, rather, within the basic family of love and source of all other love, the Trinity.

God is a community of loving intimacy of a Father emptying Himself into His Son through His Spirit of love. Such intimacy and self-emptying are returned by the Son, gifting Himself back to the Father through the same Spirit. In the Trinity, Jesus reveals to us the secret of life. Love is a call to receive one's *being* in the intimate self-surrendering of the other. In the ecstacy of "standing outside" of oneself and becoming available through the gift of love to live for the other, the Father and the Son and the Holy Spirit all come into their unique *being* as distinct, yet united, Persons within the same circle of intimate love.

"The *I* is the child of the *We*," to quote the phrase of Gabriel Marcel. God, as Trinity, is the revelation that uniqueness of persons comes only from a family of two or more persons in love. In the very self-giving of the Father to the Son and the Son to the Father, a third Person has His *being*. The Holy Spirit proceeds as the *LOVE* between the Father and the Son.

This is the fundamental truth revealed by Christ in its fullness, that at the heart of all reality, of all being, is God as a community of intimate, loving persons in which the Spirit of Love is calling two Persons into intimate "ecstatic" communion with each other. In joyful surrender, the two discover their uniqueness in their oneness. Their presence to each other as gift, a giving away in free self-surrender of each to the other, paradoxically, is a receiving of new life, new openness, that yearns still more to live as gift to the other.

God's Exploding Love

Our Christian faith assures us that the best explanation of why God has created us and this material world, so beautiful in all its variety and harmony of creations, is that the ecstatic love of the Trinity explodes outward through the same Spirit of Love to other themselves as a "pass-over" gift in creating human beings to be made participators of God's very own nature (2 P 1:4).

How exciting, and yet ever so humbling, for us to realize that we, with the whole material creation, are caught up into the trinitarian ecstasy of love. We are a part of God's joyful discovery of what it means to be uniquely a Father and a Son in the Spirit of Love.

The presence of each Divine Person to the other is a similar presence to us. As the Father is turned toward the Son in total openness, availability and vulnerability unto complete self-emptying, so the Son is turned in the same Love, the Spirit, toward the Father. That ecstatic "turning" to each other in love cannot be a different turning in love toward us. God has created us out of His ecstatic happiness that we might love also in *ecstasy* (in Greek it means to stand outside of oneself toward another in love), going out of ourselves and moving always in loving presence toward others.

God's Call

God calls us, as He called Adam and Eve in the Garden of Eden, to communicate with His Word in the Spirit of love. He allows us to share in the covenant He extended to Abraham at Haran (Gn 12:1-4; 15:1-21; 18:19), if we, too, are ready to give up all attachment through self-centeredness to earthly possessions in order to obey God's will.

God's calling of individuals is His calling to each of them to perform a work of cooperation to extend His eternal love to His collective people "of all nations." Thus, God never calls an individual to share God's life alone, but He calls a people, the "called-out" assembly, the *Qahal* (in Greek, *ekklesia*), of God to enter into His trinitarian community.

He called His Chosen People, the Israelites (Ex 3:9-10), out of the slavery of Egypt. They were in need of a *conversion*, a *metanoia*. They had to turn away from the fleshpots of Egypt to encounter Yahweh in the desert by deep faith, hope and loving obedience (Ex 12:50). God elected them as His favored people and to them He promised His faithful, protective love (Ex 19:1-9; 34:10-27).

We see that in all of God's dealings with human communities He is personally involved in issuing the call to share more intimately in His very own life and being. This can come about only by our personal and communal cooperation and continued conversion away from selfishness. Such a change of heart floods us with an experiential knowledge of God's *election*.

The New Covenant

It is, however, in the New Testament that we, who belong to Jesus, can understand how Jesus in His resurrection not only unveils how He is the fullness and the power and the glory of Yahweh through His released Spirit, but He is able to actualize God's covenant by allowing us to live in Him and receive His power and glory to bring others into God's family. The New Testament is a record of the faith of the first Christian community, the "called-out" people of God of the new covenant, as it reflects on God's actions among His people, especially in the fulfilling actions of His Son, Jesus, risen in glory and recognized by His followers to be truly God and man through His Holy Spirit.

How beautifully St. Paul summarizes our election through God's free predestination to be His holy and spotless people:

> Blessed be God the Father of our Lord Jesus Christ, who has blessed us with all the spiritual blessings of heaven in Christ. Before the world was made, he chose us, chose us in Christ, to be holy and spotless, and to live through love in his presence, determining that we should become his adopted sons, through Jesus Christ for his own kind purposes, to make us praise the glory of his grace, his free gift to us in the Beloved, in whom, through his blood, we gain our freedom, the forgiveness of our sins. Such is the richness of the grace which he has showered on us in all wisdom and insight. He has let us know the mystery of his purpose, the hidden plan he so kindly made in Christ from the beginning to act upon when the times had run their course to the end; that he would bring everything together under Christ, as head, everything in the heavens and everything on earth. And it is in him that we were claimed as God's own, chosen from the beginning, under the predetermined plan of the one who guides all things as he decides by his own will, chosen to be for his greater glory, the people who would put their hope in Christ before he came. (Ep 1:3-12)

To Bring All Things Into Fulfillment

Only in the light of Christ's resurrection and in His Spirit can we understand, not only the beginning of God's involving love toward all of us human beings, but also the end, the goal and final glorification. Jesus Christ, the perfect "image of the unseen God" (Col 1:15), in whom all things have been created, has been "called" by His Father to bring all things into fulfillment.

> As he is the Beginning,
> he was first to be born from the dead,
> so that he should be first in every way,
> because God wanted all perfection
> to be found in him
> and all things to be reconciled through him and
> for him,
> everything in heaven and everything on earth,
> when he made peace by his death on the cross.
> (Col 1:18-20)

St. Paul understood toward the end of his earthly life the fullness of what was revealed to him on the road to Damascus. We read in the letter to Colossians how Christ is the Head and the Church, the *ekklesia*, or "called-out" people of God, is His very own Body. "Before anything was created, he existed, and he holds all things in unity. Now the Church is his Body, he is its Head" (Col 1:17-18).

Christ The Recapitulator Of All Things

St. Paul arrived at his vision of God's entire plan of salvation through Jesus Christ as the one who would recapitulate or bring all things to completion after his initial vision and conversion on the road to Damascus.

"Saul, Saul, why do you persecute me?" From that first encounter with Jesus Christ, Paul met the Savior of the world as the Lord of the universe, the Cosmic Christ. He had set out to persecute the followers of the man named Jesus, who had been put to death in Jerusalem for blasphemously claiming, in substance, that He was the Son of God. But along the road to Damascus, Saul became Paul, and Jesus became for him the living Son of God, "the image of the invisible God, the first-born of every creature, because in him were created all creatures in the heavens and on earth" (Col 1:15).

16

That haunting voice seared Paul's being. It was never to be forgotten. The implications of Christ's words gradually became clearer to Paul through the years of prayerful encounter with his Lord. A steady progression in Paul's thought can be discerned in his epistles, as his Christology takes on more specific and more extensive form.

The final period of development gives us the best expression of the dimensions of Paul's cosmic Christology. Here he strives to define more precisely Christ's relationship, not only to individual human beings, but also to the whole cosmos. Christ appears as the center of unity, drawing all things back to their origins. Since the world was created for Christ (Col 1:6), it must be recapitulated or reestablished in and through Him under whose power all creatures must one day be united (see the letters to Colossians and Ephesians).

The Mystical Body Of Christ

Before we can deepen our understanding of the doctrine of the communion of saints, therefore, we must understand our oneness in love with Jesus Christ, our Head, and His Body, the Church, of which we are His members. If we abide in Him and He abides in us, we will bear great fruit in terms of loving others as He loves us (Jn 15:5-12). The power of love is to unite what has been separated or divided. It brings into harmony and unity a diversity, without destroying the differences. The more you are raised by God's Spirit to the intimate presence of God, Father, Son and Spirit, living and loving within you with an infinite love, the more you and all the saints in Christ begin to enter into communion, a union with other human beings and also all other sub-human creatures. There develops within you a genuine sense of being one with the whole world, of being open and ready to give yourself to the world in loving service in order to draw out the happiness and well-being of each creature. Strangely, the paradox of love is that the more you lose yourself for love of others to serve them, the more you find your true self in the oneness you share with them in Christ.

On June 29, 1943, Pope Pius XII issued his encyclical on the Mystical Body of Christ. In a very real way it became the foundation for the spirit of Vatican II and its thrust outward toward the world to bring it into a Christ-oneness as we human beings in Christ work with the power of the Risen Lord's Spirit. Pius XII teaches that Jesus Christ has taken a new Body complete with members. This Body he terms the *Mystical Body* or "grace-filled" Body of Christ. Christ is the Head, as St. Paul teaches. The Church is the Body. And Christians are the members of this Body. The Holy Spirit is likened to the soul of the human body for it "informs" and gives grace, especially the graces of divinization and the graces of faith, hope and love.

Through the teaching and applications of this most important encyclical, we are led away from many disconnected devotions to center more completely all our devotion and worship upon Christ, Emmanuel, God-with-us, God in relationship of most vital intimacy and deepest unity with each individual Christian. He is also God with those non-Christians who, according to the mind of Christ *ex voto*, desire to live in the kind of love that Jesus lived and taught His disciples to live. Devotions to the Sacred Heart of Jesus, adoration of the Blessed Sacrament, Christ the King, focused on aspects of Jesus Christ that presented Him as extrinsic to His followers. The doctrine of the Mystical Body presents Christ as the Head of the Body, His Church, and as the font of all graces. He is intimately, organically, united to His members, His followers.

One Organism

There are many types of organizations of intellectual beings in certain forms of unity. There can be an organization such as a bowling team. The members are united as persons living their own individual lives, yet coming together around a common goal, namely, to find recreation through bowling together. In John's Gospel, Jesus calls Himself the Good

Shepherd (Jn 10:1-18). Here we see Him as never apart from His sheep, His followers. Yet, in spite of His great love for them unto laying down His life on their behalf and their obedience to His words and commands, the Good Shepherd remains always extrinsic to the sheep.[1]

Again, in John's Gospel, Jesus likens Himself to the vine, while His members are like branches which, if they abide in Him, will bear fruit of love for each other (Jn 15:1-12). Here we see a more intimate relation of Christ to us, His members. There is an organic unity with the very same life coursing through the members as through the root and the vine. Yet the uniqueness of each member is not highlighted.

In the apt choice of Pope Pius XII's allegory of the human body, we are brought back to the example used by St. Paul to convey the deepest union between Christ, the Head, and human persons as members. The emphasis is on the one and the same life shared by the Head and the members. The Church is more than a body of individuals banded together through a common goal. Yet, the Church also has one common goal with the Head: the welfare of the entire Body unto God's glory and adoration. The Church is not a physical Body of Christ, as that born of Mary, yet it is the same historical person, God and Man, Jesus Christ, Who died for us and rose from the dead to become, through the release of His Spirit, the Head of His new Body, the Church.

There is a union of oneness and intimacy between Christ, the Head, and His members through the same life-giving Holy Spirit Who binds both the Head and the members into a singleness of Body. This same Spirit brings about, also, a union among the members as each member performs in the Body unique, vital functions for the well-being of the whole Body and the Head.

---

[1] For a good explanation of this encyclical, see Pius Parsch, *We Are Christ's Body* (Notre Dame, IN: Fides, 1962).

Unity And Diversity

Teilhard de Chardin simply describes true love as that which differentiates as it unites. This is borne out in the analogy of the human body used by St. Paul and as the basis of the teaching of the encyclical on the Mystical Body of Christ. St. Paul describes the unity and the diversity that exist in the Body of Christ, the Church:

> Just as the human body, though it is made up of many parts, is a single unit because all these parts, though many, make one body, so it is with Christ. In the one Spirit, we were all baptized, Jews, as well as Greeks, slaves, as well as citizens, and one Spirit was given to us all to drink.
>
> Nor is the body to be identified with any one of its many parts. If the foot were to say, "I am not a hand and so I do not belong to the body," would that mean that it was not a part of the body? If your whole body was just one eye, how would you hear anything? If it was just one ear, how would you smell anything?
>
> Instead of that, God put all the separate parts into the body on purpose. If all the parts were the same, how could it be a body? As it is, the parts are many, but the body is one. The eye cannot say to the hand, "I do not need you," nor can the head say to the feet, "I do not need you."
>
> What is more, it is precisely the parts of the body that seem to be the weakest which are the indispensable ones . . . and so that there may not be disagreements inside the body, but that each part may be equally concerned for all the others. If one part is hurt, all parts are hurt with it. If one part is given special honor, all parts enjoy it.
>
> Now you together are Christ's body, but each of you is a different part of it. (1 Co 12:12-27)

All Graces Come Through Christ, The Head

If we wish to understand the intercessory power of human persons, the saints, both those living on this earth, as St. Paul so often calls his fellow Christians, and those who have gone into eternal life, to aid other members of the Body, we must clearly understand in the doctrine concerning the Church as Christ's Body that only Christ, the Head, is the Source of all grace.

In the allegory of the vine and the branches, Jesus clearly teaches us that without Him we are nothing but dried-up branches, fit only to be burned. ". . . for cut off from me you can do nothing" (Jn 15:5). We are, however, to ask, but only in His Name (Jn 15:16), then the Father will give us whatever we ask Him.

Pius XII clearly teaches this in his encyclical when he writes:

> Jesus Christ . . . merited for us an unspeakable abundance of graces. These graces he might himself, had he so chosen, have bestowed directly upon the whole human race, but he willed to do this by means of a visible Church in which men would be united, and through which they would cooperate with him in distributing the divine fruit of redemption.[2]

We are the visible part of the Body of Christ, the "representation" of the historical Christ in our time and place in history, to "cooperate with Him (Christ) in distributing the divine fruit of redemption." We have gifts to bring unto the fulfillment of the Body, the Church. As St. Paul expresses it: "There is a variety of gifts, but always the same Spirit; there are all sorts of service to be done, but always to the same Lord; working in all sorts of different ways in different people; it is the same God who is working in all of them. The

---

[2] *Mystici Corporis*, C.T.S. Edition (London, 1943), n. 12.

in which the Spirit is given to each person is for a good purpose" (1 Co 12:4-7).

The Bridegroom And The Bride

Something vital to our relationship to Jesus Christ is lacking in the analogy of the human body to describe our oneness with the Head, Jesus Christ. It is this other element that will allow us to penetrate deeper into the true understanding of the communion of saints. What is not highlighted in the analogy with a human body is that, as individual members of Christ, we have free will. We can, alas, freely refuse to allow the life of Christ, Who opens us up through His Spirit to the uncreated energies of trinitarian love, to be transformative in our daily lives.

By Baptism, we are "incorporated" into Christ. We "have been stamped with the seal of the Holy Spirit of the Promise" (Ep 1:13). We can never lose this belonging to the trinitarian family, for this is God's gift to us. We cannot, by our sinfulness, force God to undo His constant, everlasting, trinitarian loving relationship in His New Covenant, to which He freely and forever has committed Himself. St. Paul describes the full gratuitous gift of God's salvation offered to us:

> But God loved us with so much love that he was generous with his mercy; when we were dead through our sins, he brought us to life with Christ — it is through grace that you have been saved — and raised us up with him and gave us a place with him in heaven, in Christ Jesus . . . Because it is by grace that you have been saved, through faith, not by anything of your own, but by a gift from God, not by anything you have done, so that nobody can claim the credit. We are God's work of art, created in Christ Jesus to live the good life as from the beginning he had meant us to live it (Ep 2:4-10).

Yet, all too often in our personal history and in the communal experience of the Church, we see how we can become "dead" members, who refuse to live by God's grace. Yet, we also know our human dignity that, by God's free election (Gn 1:26), we have been made according to His own image and likeness. Through our rational gifts and free will, we can come to know God and His infinite love for us in the Incarnate Word, Jesus Christ, through His revelation, and we can surrender to Christ's headship as our Lord and Savior.

St. Paul offers to us the complement to his analogy of the human body by giving us the analogy of Christ as the Bridegroom and of the Church and us, as the individual members of the Church, as the Bride. Here we move beyond God's unilateral relationship to us through the revelation in the person of Jesus Christ to enter into the most intimate relationship that we human beings naturally can conceive, that of a husband and wife who, in total availability, mutuality and in self-sacrificing gift of one to the other, live in loving union. This is how Paul describes pastorally how a husband and wife should love each other as Christ, the Bridegroom, loves His Bride, the Church:

> Give way to one another in obedience to Christ. Wives should regard their husbands as they regard the Lord, since as Christ is head of the Church and saves the whole body, so is a husband the head of his wife; and as the Church submits to Christ, so should wives to their husbands, in everything. Husbands should love their wives just as Christ loved the Church and sacrificed himself for her to make her holy. He made her clean by washing her in water with a form of words, so that when he took her to himself she would be glorious, with no speck or wrinkle or anything like that, but holy and faultless. In the same way, husbands must love their wives as they love their own bodies, for a man to love his wife is for him to love himself. A man never hates his own body, but he feeds it and looks after it; and that is the way Christ treats the Church, because it is his body — and we are

its living parts. . . . This mystery has many implications, but I am saying it applies to Christ and the Church (Ep 5:21-32).

Jesus, The Lover Of Mankind

The use of the bridal analogy to express the most intimate self-giving love between Yahweh and His Chosen People and between Christ and His Church is not original to Paul. Basically, God is the "Lover" of the human race, the great *Philanthropos* (in Greek). Jesus is the image of the unseen God (Col 1:15) and He best mirrors in human form the perfection of God as Lover when He dies for love of us. Is it any wonder the most consistent and powerful metaphor used in Scripture to describe God's burning love for His people and for each individual who enters into the kingdom of heaven is that of God, and above all, Christ, as the Bridegroom?

We read in the Old Testament, especially after the exile when God renewed His covenant, how God is the Bridegroom and His chosen people are His Bride. Hosea is the prophet of such an espousal:

> I will betroth you to myself forever,
> betroth you with integrity and justice,
> with tenderness and love;
> I will betroth you to myself with faithfulness,
> and you will come to know Yahweh (Hos 2:21-22).

Isaiah also beautifully describes such an intimate, bridal relationship between God and His people, Israel: "...and as the bridegroom rejoices in his bride, so will your God rejoice in you" (Is 62:5).

But the peak of bridal mysticism is found in the beautiful *Song of Songs* of the Old Testament. Early Christian exegetes, beginning with Origen and St. Gregory of Nyssa, used a method of interpretation called *typology* that saw this sacred book to be not only a revelation of Yahweh in bridal union with Israel, His Bride, but of God's passionate love for all human beings through Christ as the Bridegroom and the Church as the Bride and each individual member baptized into the Body, the Church, to be in bridal oneness with Christ.[3]

I Am Black . . . But Lovely

In a mystical interpretation of this key text of the *Song of Songs*, the bride stands for the fervent Christian who, in spite of past sins and present failings, knows she has become beautiful through the workings of Jesus' Spirit. The bride shows the delicate balance between what she is without Christ and, yet, what she is now through His loving grace. The deeper you go into your unconscious being, the more you will discover the sin and death that have not yet been conquered by the new life Christ comes to give you.

By confronting the false ego, you bring the perfect love of God, as experienced in the intimate, indwelling presence of Christ, to heal the fears that drive you into the dark world of unreality. "In love there can be no fear, but fear is driven out by perfect love" (1 Jn 4:18). As the darkness of your sinful nature lifts before the transfiguring light of the indwelling Christ, you begin to see that you also radiate a new beauty, a sharing in Christ's beauty.

The Good News that Jesus reveals to us and makes possible through the sanctifying power of the Spirit's grace is that you and I can be continually lifted up into greater oneness with Christ, our Bridegroom, and His Spirit reveals that, through our cooperation, God's grace has truly transformed us into persons who please the heart of Christ and His Father. Christ, the Bridegroom, can address us as His Beloved. He confesses: "You ravish my heart" (Sg 4:9).

---

[3] For a Christological interpretation of the *Song of Songs*, see my book: *Singers of the New Song* (Notre Dame, IN: Ave Maria Press, 1985).

A Oneness In Christ

We know through the Spirit, the "soul" of the Body of Christ, how beautiful we are in Christ's transforming love. We not only can return to Him a similar gift of ourselves in self-surrendering love, but we can, in a *synergy*, or a mutual working with Christ, go forth to be a gift of loving service to others. We can with Christ, through His Spirit, build the Body of Christ. We can fashion with Christ, the Word, in whom all things are made (Jn 1:2), this universe into a unity amidst maximum diversity and bring to completion God's initial creation of a community of love in unity and diversity.

By our Baptism and regeneration by the Holy Spirit, we are now one with Christ. With St. Paul, we too can confess: "I have been crucified with Christ, and I live now not with my own life, but with the life of Christ who lives in me. The life I now live in this body I live in faith: faith in the Son of God who loved me and who sacrificed himself for my sake. I cannot bring myself to give up God's gift. . . ." (Ga 2:19-21).

Such a life with Christ in mystical union gives us the highest dignity to live by and the possessing in highest freedom of our true self. Only such a person has become free enough by the Holy Spirit of the risen Lord to take his/her life and freely dispose of it as a free, loving gift in service to others.

Thus, we see the necessity of first viewing God's complete plan of reality, if we are to understand accurately the doctrine of the communion of saints. We have seen the intercommunion within the Trinity as the beginning and end of all reality. Out of such intimate, self-emptying love of Father and Son through binding love of the Holy Spirit, Who unites what is unique and diverse, we can believe that God's love explodes outward to create this material world. At the center, He places man and woman to become by their free consent co-creators with God of this world.

The Holy Spirit brings about a unity within the Body, the

Church. St. Paul describes the call of ourselves to unity through the workings of the Holy Spirit:

> I, the prisoner in the Lord, implore you, therefore, to lead a life worthy of your vocation. Bear with one another charitably, in complete selflessness, gentleness and patience. Do all you can to preserve the unity of the Spirit by the peace that binds you together. There is one Body, one Spirit, just as you were all called into one and the same hope when you were called. There is one Lord, one faith, one baptism, and one God who is Father of all, over all, through all and within all (Ep 4:1-6).

Living intimately in oneness with Jesus Christ by the grace of the Spirit, we are called to co-create with the Trinity a unity in the Body of Christ, the Church, which is the leaven to raise the entire world into new life, a new creation. Paul again exhorts his fellow-Christians: "If our life in Christ means anything to you, if love can persuade at all, or the Spirit that we have in common, or any tenderness and sympathy, then be united in your convictions and united in your love, with a common purpose and a common mind... There must be no competition among you, no conceit, but everybody is to be self-effacing. Always consider the other person to be better than yourself, so that nobody thinks of his own interests first, but everybody thinks of other people's interests ahead. In your minds, you must be the same as Christ Jesus" (Ph 2:1-5).

To Be Where You Love

Now we can advance to consider a new presence of love that surpasses all confinement of space and time. For most human beings, space and time are only measurements of accomplishments. In reality, space and time, our historical moments now, should become the backdrop against which we grow into our true identity in our oneness with and in Jesus

Christ. The poet, W. H. Auden, profoundly describes space and time in terms of meaningful, loving relationships:

Space is the Whom our loves are needed by,
Time is our choice of How to love and Why.[4]

Our Christian teaching assures us in a faith-vision that our God is a loving, concerned God. We are not tossed into a time of history and a geographical place like flotsam on the ocean. God has called us into being in a historical time and place. There He promises to meet us and to invite us to enter into a covenant friendship in order to share with us His very own life and being.

To be human is to hear God's continued call in the depths of our being in what Scripture calls our "heart." He calls us in a vocation to cooperate more progressively, by the power of His Son and Holy Spirit, to become what we now are not. He calls us, also, to assist in "mid-wifing" into being the entire universe from what it is now. We are nomadic people stretching toward our true homeland, "living among foreigners in the Dispersion" (1 P 1:1). Yet, we are called "by the provident purpose of God, the Father, to be made holy by the Spirit, obedient to Jesus Christ and sprinkled with his blood" (1 P 1:2).

By truly passing over from isolation and self-centeredness, by living in true, self-emptying love through self-sacrificing service toward others, we not only enter into our true oneness in Christ, but we cooperate to bring other human beings and the entire material creation into a wholeness in Christ, into "a new creation" (2 Co 5:17) as we live in Christ.

True love, therefore, has the unique power to catch up space and time and transform them into an experience of two persons becoming one in spacelessness that knows no harshness of ticking time. In love you burst the limitations of confining space and time. You soar through the firmaments

---

[1] W.H. Auden, "For the Time Being," in *The Collected Poetry*, ed. Edward Mendelson (NY: Random House, 1945), p. 447.

of past, present and future as you learn to rest in the ever-abiding *now* moment of loving union with God and neighbor. No place can hold you within its painful grasp as you stretch to touch the ecstasy of eternity.

St. John of the Cross explains how love transcends the limits of our earthly bodies:

> The soul lives where it loves rather than in the body which it animates, because it has not its life in the body, but rather gives it to the body and lives through love in that which it loves.[5]

You and I have surely experienced the truth of this statement in the most beautiful moments of our human loves and in our love of God. By the death and resurrection of Jesus Christ, we can now receive His same Holy Spirit of love, Who brought the risen Lord into a new existence that destroyed the boundaries and limitations of time and space.

The resurrection of Jesus Christ is a new beginning which brings to an end the dominations of historical time and space. And yet, His resurrection happens within the orbit of earthly time and space. God mysteriously has now entered into the history of humanity and from inside is setting about to destroy sin, corruption and death. This is done completely in Jesus but, gradually through His risen presence in His living members who become leaven, God speaks to raise all of humanity and the whole of creation into a sharing of Jesus' new life.

Now, with this as the background, we can advance and prayerfully seek to understand such a "new creation" in Christ that makes possible the communion of saints. We are dealing with something much greater than whether the saints in heaven can intercede for us as we offer our prayers through their loving hands to God. We are dealing with the

---

[5] St. John of the Cross: *The Spiritual Canticle*, in *The Collected Works of St. John of the Cross*; tr. Kieran Kavanaugh, O.C.D. and Otilio Rodriguez, O.C.D. (Wash., D.C.: Institute of Carmelite Studies, 1973), p. 441.

essence of Christianity. St. Paul's vision of a new creation in Christ offers us a suitable conclusion to this chapter and a preparation for those chapters to follow:

> And for anyone who is in Christ, there is a new creation; the old creation has gone, and now the new one is here. It is all God's work. It was God who reconciled us to himself through Christ and gave us the work of handing on this reconciliation. In other words, God in Christ was reconciling the world to himself, not holding men's faults against them, and as he has entrusted to us the news that they are reconciled. So we are ambassadors for Christ; it is as though God were appealing through us and, the appeal that we make in Christ's name is: to be reconciled to God. (2 Co 5:17-21)

Chapter Two

COMMUNION WITH THE SPIRIT WORLD

Are you familiar with the meaning of a *hologram*? It is a part of an image that, when illuminated by a laser beam, seems suspended in three-dimensional space and, as a piece, contains the entire image. I believe this can be a most helpful image through modern science to convey to us what we have stressed in the preceding chapter on the Mystical Body of Christ. We may be just a simple piece of the whole plan of God which embraces, not only every human person created according to God's image and likeness, but also every atom of matter created by the same loving God. But we also contain, in God's view and in potentiality, the whole universe. We can never be separated from this gigantic universe.

God created the stars and the oceans, the animals and human beings all to exist in a dynamic universe of infinite relationships to each other and to God. Everything in the cosmos is inter-connected and moves in a harmonious wholeness. Each part has its proper place within the universe.

Yet, as human beings, created out of the Trinity's personalized love to be participators in God's very own nature, we share in the ability to grow in consciousness through human freedom. We are empowered by God's Spirit to be the love-spark that can ignite the whole and lead the entire universe with God's graceful power into a unity of diversity, into the fullness of the glorified, total Body of Christ. We have, therefore, the power to "enspirit" the matter of the universe into a unity of one body—that of the total Christ in whom, by our Christian faith, "all things were created in the heavens and on the earth" (Col 1:16).

Through our first creation into existence as human beings, we are oriented toward communion, a union with all God's creatures. We possess the whole universe within the microcosmos of our individual material selves. Through our second creation into the triune family of love, our Baptism into Jesus Christ, we are already one with all other members of the Body of Christ, the Church, and potentially already oriented toward a oneness with all human beings as our brothers and sisters in Christ, Who makes us all one family through His Spirit of love, sharing with Christ the very nature of God, Trinity.

As we move away from a simplistic, mechanistic view of God's creation and enter into a world of mystery, we enter into a world of exciting movement, flux and interrelatedness of all things. How much truer this is when we consider the unity already experienced by faith between ourselves as a part of the Body of Christ, the Church and all other members. St. Paul writes: "All baptized in Christ, you have all clothed yourselves in Christ, and there are no more distinctions between Jew and Greek, slave and free, male and female, but all of you are one in Christ Jesus. Merely by belonging to Christ you are the posterity of Abraham, the heirs he was promised" (Ga 3:27-29).

Communion With The Spirit World

Now we turn to our relationships with the world of spirits, with those human beings, especially our loved ones, parents, husband, wife, son, daughter, brother or sister, friends who have died and entered into the mysterious eternal life, along with the angelic spirits. Can we communicate with them? Can we help them by our prayers? Can, especially, our dearest friends, who have loved us intimately during the time we have lived with them on this earth, and the holy, "successful" human beings whom the Church calls "the saints" in glory, help us?

The desire to commune with such spiritual beings is a very human universal wish. Can we say that we have ever loved others enough or received enough love from our loved ones? We always will stretch out for new tomorrows, so full of the dreams of greater oneness in loving self-giving. We wish for more happiness and joy and know from human experiences that such cannot be ours in continued increase, except through communication unto communion.

Yet, all of us have experienced the cruel and total certainty of death. Old age brings about a slow deterioration that can promise only a final death and end to the only existence we have known while journeying on this earth. Just as we have begun to savor life with relish and contentment, death leers its hideous face to remind us that all will one day be under its control. Death snatches our loved ones from us and leaves us with an agonizing void and loneliness.

We rightly bereave the death of our loved ones because death is so radical, so complete. The whole earthly person, whom we have loved, is dead and gone from this earthly existence forever. We, too, have died somewhat in the loss of the beloved. But all human beings of all times and cultures must always ask the question: Does anything of my beloved remain beyond my memories? Has the dead person completely disappeared as the setting sun seems to be swallowed up in the darkness of the horizon?

A New Vision

Our habitual way of regarding those who have died and our relationships with them has been posited upon the distinction between and separation of soul and body. We believe the soul cannot really die since, by its very nature, it is immortal. It can only be the body of the human person that dies. The body is separated from the soul in death and it is that beloved's human body that is thought to be placed into a coffin and buried into the earth or cremated and changed into ashes. At the last judgment, most of us believe, there will be a gathering of the body from the dust and ashes and a reunion with the soul that has been living all this time, before the general resurrection of the dead at the end of this world, in a spiritual world of three possible "places," respectively called heaven, purgatory and hell.

We are in need of a new way of expressing the same faith about life immediately after physical death and the possibility of communing with the departed. The Bible never sees the soul as separable from the corporality of the body. Modern thought — tapping into insights from the biblical concepts of *body*, as referring always to the entire human person in his/her existence on earth or in the life to come, as well as from psychology and the understanding of human consciousness and holistic integration of all body, soul and spirit levels of relationships — concurs with the biblical holistic view of body and soul.

Entering Into The Mysterious Presence Through Love

At the moment of death, we and our loved ones and all other human persons enter into a new life beyond death. We live and die and, yet, we still live as the same persons with the same consciousness, the same relationships we had while living on this earth. If this is true, why does such a vision and truth not offer to us on earth the possibility of communing with the departed in a deeper and more loving way?

Surely God's revelation, through the Church's constant teaching and liturgical practices of praying for the dead, shows us that there is, first of all, a continuous life after death. It shows us how we can be channels of God's healing love toward those who reach out from beyond this vale of tears to love us with God's very own love in them.

Pointless Questions

When we approach death and the possibility of our continued communion with the departed solely with our minds, we will always lose the most important elements of the Church's teaching on the possibility of continued communion and become lost in speculating about what kind of a body we will have, especially when the body is "rejoined" with the soul. This approach, more than any other, has prevented us from entering into true communication and continued growth in love with our departed. We have cut off from ourselves the greatest intercessory power of the departed in their loving activities in our earthly lives and a most essential manner of even now experiencing the power of the Risen Jesus coming to our "rescue" through His members, those who already are standing with greater understanding and humility within His glorious body of the "saints."

St. Paul's advice is still relevant for us today:

> Someone may ask, "How are dead people raised, and what sort of body do they have when they come back?" They are stupid questions. Whatever you sow in the ground has to die before it is given new life and the thing that you sow is not what is going to come; you sow a bare grain, say of wheat or something like that, and then, God gives it the sort of body that he has chosen: each sort of seed gets its own sort of body. (1 Co 15:35-38)

Because we tend to place all human beings into three "objective" places upon their death, namely, they either "go to "heaven or purgatory or to hell, we make it most difficult to live in the interpersonal relationships between those who still live on this earth and those who have died. We easily distinguish between those who have died in Christ and are the "saints" in glory, still members of the Body of Christ, but now living in the *Church Triumphant*, and those who have died and are members of the *Church Suffering*, who are in need of greater purification before they enter into membership in the Church Triumphant. We Christians, who have not yet died, live in the *Church Militant*, for we are still battling sin and death on this earth.

That there exists a different "presence" to Christ, the Head of His Body, the Church, cannot be denied in such thinking. But such objectivization tends to make those on earth even more separated from those who have already entered into eternal life. It also makes all relationships with those who are "in hell" impossible.

A Contemplative View

When the Church is vibrant with deeply contemplative Christians, the understanding of the communion between the living and the dead becomes a great, living reality. The contemplative lives on a deeper plane of reality, seeing no great chasm separating them from their living neighbors for whom they intercede before the throne of God. Such Christians feel united also in prayer with all the departed, the saints, angels and those not quite brought into the fullness of God's glory through sufficient healing of earth's hurtful relationships, even those in the state of complete alienation from God, in the state of hell.

Such contemplatives live on this earth through deep faith, hope and love and are daily aware they are in union with the indwellling Trinity. God is invisible but, nonetheless, very real to them. Matter does not oppose spirit, so they easily live in the presence of all the angels and human beings living on the face of the earth and those who have departed and now live in a new spiritual presence to those on earth.

The love of Christ in the contemplative burns to win all

to Christ. One wants to share the riches of Christ with all creatures. If while on earth, St. Paul burned with a desire to become all things to all men and women to win them for Christ, how much more does he, now in heaven, burn with the love of Christ in him to intercede for all of us? The Church has always taught doctrinally and devotionally in the cult to the saints, and through the liturgical prayers on behalf of the saints, that there is communication between the living in this life and those living in Christ in the life after death.

Communication With The Departed

From the earliest Christian times, the living on this earth honored the memory of those who died in Christ. The faithful were sure that the mutual contact they enjoyed by praying for each other when alive could not be broken even by death. Origen speaks often of martyrs who stand before the altar of God with the angels to support our prayers. Martyrs in the first four centuries were honored as sharing in the Kingdom of Heaven a special intercessory power in their oneness with Christ for Whom they died. P. Styger in his excavations of the catacombs of San Sebastiano in Rome has brought to light graffiti of the 3rd century scratched on stone by pilgrims who at the graves of Saints Peter and Paul begged to obtain their intercession.

It is interesting to note that in the Byzantine Liturgy of St. John Chrysostom, the priest prays in a way similarly found in all early liturgical rites of the Church:

> Moreover, we offer You this spiritual bloodless sacrifice for our forefathers in the faith who have gone to their rest, for the fathers, patriarchs, prophets, apostles, preachers, evangelists, martyrs, confessors, ascetics and for every just soul that has died in the faith . . . and especially for our most holy, most pure, most blessed and glorious Lady, the Mother of God and ever-virgin Mary.

37

This prayer has meaning in the light of the Christian faith-vision that the faithful gather to celebrate the Liturgy in union with the heavenly courts of angels and saints and all those who have died in the faith of Christ. Around the heavenly altar, there is only the Body of Christ. He is the Head. The living, on earth or in eternal life, are the members, yet all are united in love and grace.

The many icons found throughout a Byzantine church, on the iconostasis or screen that separates the people from the Holy of Holies, on stands, on the walls, up above in the cupolas, call the faithful vividly to this realization of the Church Militant uniting with the Church Triumphant and the Church Suffering (in the afterlife). All are members of the Body of Christ, but each group manifests a different level of "life in Christ."

Such prayers for Mary the Mother of God and the saints of old could mean that the faithful implore God that the blessed may join with the living faithful in this liturgical sacrifice. It is also a prayer of thanksgiving to God for their glory and victory. And, it is a plea that the Lord have mercy on the praying community that asks this through the saints' intercession.

Doctrine Of The Communion Of Saints

Therefore, we see that, in the first five centuries of Christianity, the doctrine of the communion of saints evolved. Scholars who have researched the phrase "I believe in the *communion of saints*" trace the various meanings that evolved around this phrase.[1] The first meaning around the 4th

---

[1] The most complete research is found as the doctoral thesis of Dr. Stephen Benko: *The Meaning of Sanctorum Communio* (Naperville, IL: Alex R. Allenson, Inc., 1964).

century understood *sanctorum* as neuter plural. Communion meant a participation in one common reality or else the entering into a communication with others. Therefore, the first meaning was understood as "holy things," namely, Christians, in order to become holy, need to participate in the holy sacraments, especially Baptism and the Eucharist.

Gradually, the phrase came to mean those who have participated in the holy things and have become holy. In their sharing in the resurrectional glory of their Head, Jesus Christ, the saints enjoy a powerful, intercessory position to offer the prayers of the faithful on earth to the Head, Jesus Christ. St. Paul's writings show us how he used the phrase, *the saints*, to refer to all Christians on earth, sanctified already to some degree by God's predilection and call and by the reception and living out of the sacrament of Baptism by the individual Christian.

Thus, it was a natural step in the next centuries for the phrase to refer to the belief that death does not separate us on earth from the great and holy saints who intercede for us before Christ. It also referred to those who have died in Christ and, yet, were in need of healing after death. This basic belief is acted out in devotions to the deceased as the living ones on earth intercede to gain grace for those undergoing purifications in the afterlife. It is also found in the official prayers of the Church, in the burial services of the departed and the continued prayers for their purification.

Such mutual communication between the living and the deceased in heaven or in purgatory stemmed from the bondedness of all Christians, through Baptism, sharing in the priesthood of Christ. Such active intercession on the part of those living on earth does not take away from the sole high-priestly intercession of Jesus Christ before the Heavenly Throne. It is a sharing in Christ's power of intercession as found in the first epistle of St. Peter: "But you are a chosen race, a royal priesthood, a consecrated nation, a people set apart to sing the praises of God who called you out of the darkness into his wonderful light" (1 P 2:9).

A Continued Growth In Love After Death

Our faith, therefore, convinces us that all the members of the Body of Christ, on earth or in the afterlife in the state of heaven or purgatory, are interrelated and continue to live out the "holy things," what is symbolized and effected by the ongoing living out of our Baptism into Christ and becoming eucharist to each other, regardless of what is the state of the journey unto holiness of any member.

If the saints, therefore, continue to be active, with full consciousness, memory and understanding of our needs and can exercise acts of love and compassion toward us still in this exile, what does this important teaching of the communion of the saints have still to tell us? Would it be beyond our Christian faith to believe that the saints, therefore, through their loving concern for all the members of the Body of Christ, including each of us in our many needs, can actually grow in greater love, as they lovingly seek to serve all others in the building up of the total Body of Christ?

Can one, who loves God in the life to come, not want to share that love, even want to become involved with those in greatest need? Each act of love, each concerned thought for one of us on this earth by one who knows the Lord "face-to-face" should push that person to a new level of human growth, of human consciousness of God's beauty both in him/herself and in the life of the one for whom the saint intercedes.

We would cease being human, made "according to the image and likeness of God," if we could not grow continuously toward infinity in ever-increasing love. If we were to meet Christ as the Omega Point in a completed state of fixity, what would the love of God and neighbor mean in such a vacuum? Would it not mean that God would also stop manifesting Himself in self-emptying through the members of the Body of Christ if all members with their Head would cease from self-giving love and service?

Yet, what an injustice that the habitual image used of

eternal happiness is that of a long, eternal sleep. "Eternal rest grant unto them, O Lord," the Requiem Mass for centuries resounded. We failed to realize that scriptural "rest" is not inactivity. It is the stretching out toward greater completion and integration of the multiplied perfections of God in His creation into new and more intense oneness of love.

T. S. Eliot beautifully describes God's eternal life as the source of all created life, as a *dance* at the still point of the turning world that would be a poetic description of the state of heaven where the Body of Christ is always growing in complexity and in unity through the loving service on behalf of each other by the members of Christ.

> At the still point of the turning world
> Neither flesh nor fleshless,
> Neither from nor towards,
> At the still point, there the dance is,
> But neither arrest nor movement.
> And do not call it fixity,
> Where past and future are gathered.
> Neither movement from nor towards,
> Neither ascent nor decline.
> Except for the point, the still point,
> There would be no dance,
> And there is only dance.
> I can only say, there we have been;
> But I cannot say where.
> And I cannot say how long,
> For that is to place it in time.[2]

Love Never Ends

What we have described as the possibility of continued growth among the saints, as they lovingly seek to serve all the children of God, would apply also to those in purgatory.

---

[2] T.S. Eliot, *Burnt Norton* from his *Four Quartets* (N.Y.: Harcourt Brace Jovanovich, Inc., 1943).

But this truth follows only when we see it clearly in the case of those whom the love of Christ drives forward to extend his "kenotic" or self-emptying love for His Bride, His Body, the Church. We will deal with the therapy-growth in a chapter on purgatory and also on hell and the love-growth in us as we lovingly serve those in need in the life after death.

What we are presenting here is not a modern, new look in life after death. It is one of the incisive insights that many of the Eastern Christian mystical theologians as Origen, St. Gregory of Nyssa and St. Gregory of Nazianzus, St. Maximus the Confessor, and St. Symeon the New Theologian, to name only a few, give us of a continued progress for humans in the life to come. We have stated that for those saints in the state called heaven, perfection or holiness does not consist in static possession, in rest, or a continued looking upon God in an objective "beatific vision."

St. Gregory of Nyssa argues that, since God's beauty that beckons human beings is limitless, the desire in them must also be limitless. There will always be a paradoxical tension between motion and stability, between loving union and passion for greater oneness. He writes:

> . . . the soul keeps rising ever higher and higher, stretching with its desire for heavenly things to those that are before (Ph 3:13), as the Apostle tells us and, thus, it will always continue to soar ever higher. For, because of what it has already attained, the soul does not wish to abandon the heights that lie beyond it. And, thus, the soul moves ceaselessly upwards, always reviving its tension for its onward flight by means of the progress it has already realized. Indeed, it is only spiritual activity that nourishes its force by exercise; it does not slacken its tension by action, but rather increases it.[3]

---

[3] St. Gregory Nyssa, *Life of Moses:* PG 44:405D, cited in *From Glory to Glory*, ed. Jean Danielou and H. Musurillo (N.Y.: Scribner's 1961), p. 150.

St. Paul beautifully describes the qualities of true love, which will be the authentic measure of any human person's greatness in the kingdom of heaven:

> Love does not come to an end. But, if there are gifts of prophecy, the time will come when they must fail, or the gift of languages, it will not continue forever. . . . In short, there are three things that last: faith, hope and love, and the greatest of these is love. (1 Co 13:8,13)

But we have already seen in the teaching of the Mystical Body of Christ that, according to Paul, "if one part is hurt, all parts are hurt with it. If one part is given special honor, all parts enjoy it" (1 Co 12:26). Could we ever imagine that the state of heaven would isolate us from the poor and suffering of this world? Would we enjoy eternal happiness and love of God without also seeking to love others, especially the members of God's created family, His children, who are hurting?

Mary, The Handmaid Of The Lord

The more the saints in heaven are filled with the Spirit of God's love and are being constantly transformed into ever more beautiful, loving persons, the more they are set free to give themselves as a gift of loving service to others. Is it any wonder that the Church and its faithful have from earliest times venerated Mary's greatness and associated that greatness with her loving concern for all the children of God?

Mary, as she is asked to become the Mother of Jesus, the Savior, is declared full of grace by the angel of Gabriel. She gives her *fiat* to serve the Lord as His lowly handmaid (Lk 1:38). How she must have grown in that love as she served the Word made flesh in the thirty years at Nazareth! At the foot of the cross, how that grace, that surrendering love reached its fullest desire to possess and be possessed by that Word! And after 2,000 human years, according to our reckoning, what *now*, in her presence to Jesus Christ and her desire to serve him in all the children of God, must be her fullness of grace!

I often think of the parallel of a mother with a retarded child. How the retarded child calls out more love from the mother than the mother is challenged to give to her other "normal" children! Her love is so unselfish and, yet, any such mother will tell the world how much she has received in real growth in love and human self-realization. There is a constant tradition in the Church that has believed and acted on that belief that Mary in glory is very present among us, her children in exile. She is constantly interceding for God's children, especially in her loving concern with those in greatest need.

As a priest involved in reconciling the broken ones of this earth who come to me in the sacrament of reconciliation, I begin to see the awfulness of sin as a darkening of human persons' ability to see God because, like retarded children of God, they never came to know the beauties of God in Jesus Christ. Does it matter whether it was deliberately or indeliberately on their part that they grew up never grasping "the breadth and the length, the height and the depth" (Ep 3:18) of the love of Christ?

One person was forced to grow up in a broken family and at an early age was on the streets in gangs who knew only violence and hatred for the wealthy. Another was spoiled by parents and never knew self-discipline, but only self-indulgence. One other was brought up on an Irish Jansenism that feared sex. I often ask God how much their "sins" are deliberate acts of turning away from God and how much was the responsibility of their society. Here are broken people who need the healing love of Jesus Christ.

We can see today the power of history and culture to keep a whole nation tied to a religion that militates against Christianity or a nation that persecutes any freedom of religion. We see the evils of Christianity in the past that were used by the wealthy classes to forget to hear the cries of the poor.

44

Love Begets Love

Can we not believe that the saints, and even our loved ones, even though they have entered into the necessary therapy needed to bring Christ's love into their earthly experiences that were filled with selfishness, seek to help us? In a real way, they also need us in order to allow their great love for God to unfold and be actualized in a new, expanded consciousness.

Are they not comparable to highly developed persons with skills which they wish to share with us? They have graduated with their Ph.D. degrees in how to love God and neighbor and wish to teach us on this earth how to read, write and do simple problems in the only course worth passing in this life.

All who believe in Jesus Christ are living members of His Body and this presence transcends the temporal and spatial limitations of our imperfect existence on this earth. Someday we will understand how our loved ones, also the angels and saints and the billions of masked saints, who never reached canonization, were most influential in helping us to love God while we journeyed on this earth. And we will rejoice when we discover how our loving intercession on this earth has helped those in need in their purification process in the life after death.

This is a small hint of the importance of this creedal statement: "I believe in the communion of saints."

Chapter Three

COMMUNION BETWEEN THE LIVING AND THE DEAD

We have seen that communion of saints embraces the powerful intercession of the angels and saints on our behalf as pilgrims still on this earth, as well as intercessory prayer between the living on earth for each other. We need now to extend this communication because of mutual communion with Jesus Christ, the Head of the Body, the Church, to that between the saints, the living on this earth and those departed living in the purification stage called *purgatory*.

All of us have surely lost a loved one, a father or mother, husband or wife, son or daughter, brother or sister, or dear friend. And with absolute certainty we, too, still living on this earth, will physically die and continue no longer to exist in the only manner we are familiar with now. So it is natural for us to ask what sort of existence do our departed loved ones enjoy now? What existence awaits each of us after our earthly death? Is there communion now between us still living on this earth and our departed loved ones? Can we communicate with them and help them as they undergo the therapy of their past weaknesses, sinful habits, painful experiences, unresolved fears, guilts, worries? Can others help us when we reach the intermediate stage between this present life and that of eternal life called heaven? This intermediate stage in the Church's long teaching has come to be known by the word *purgatory.*

The Catholic and Orthodox Churches have long taught the consoling truth that there exists a state of further purification after death known as purgatory. Above all, we can be consoled that we, still living, can be in vital, loving contact and communion with our departed loved ones. When our dear ones die, they still live, and death does not break the possibility of our living in communication and loving service toward them.

The Church has taught from earliest liturgical practices, in all Eastern and Western liturgies, in funeral and commemorative services on behalf of the deceased, as well as in daily commemorations, that we can help them by offering "suffrages" on their behalf. The Council of Florence in the 15th century defined *suffrages* as "the sacrifice of the Mass, prayers, alms and other religious activities which, according to the laws and customs of the Church, the faithful normally offer."

The Real World Of God's Love

We need, in this matter, to avoid spectacular and selfish "exploitation" of our departed loved ones, by being guided by the Church's long-standing teaching on communion between the living and the dead. The first step in our living in God's reality is to destroy our false ideas, which so often have come to us through paganism and a faulty theology. We tend so easily to create idols as a security so we can block out the terrifying reality of death. But all too often this stems from a defective view of death that tends to remove us from our departed loved ones and our mission to help them through a lively communion with them in loving service.

Our tinker-toy constructions need to be disassembled. We need to push ourselves into God's real world and the world in which the departed loved ones now live. Therefore, the first thing necessary, if we are to move into God's objective order and live by deeper faith and love toward our loved ones, is to get rid of our pagan, negative views of death. We have all been brought up to cling to our own concepts of life and happiness learned from our life experience. Our physical death is seen as the greatest enemy to any future life. Death seems, according to our fears, to be the end of all life. We die, period.

The best way to cope with this invincible enemy, death, is to amuse ourselves with distractions, so we don't have to think much about death, until it is completely inevitable. Separation of body and soul allows us not to take death seriously as something that happens to our whole person but merely to our physical bodies. We need to see that death is not merely the wages of sin, but that, as the Eastern Fathers believed, physical death could have happened even without sin as a part of greater growth and life.

A New, Positive View Of Purgatory

Theologians, through superior studies on biblical theology, aided by a holistic view of the human person through semitic spirituality and modern psychology, are bringing new insights to the traditional teaching on purgatory. They are questioning the accent placed from medieval theology on the soul separated from the body, then imprisoned and subjugated to a punishment of physical fire that is, not only the pain of sense, but the pain of the damned, the temporary privation of the vision of God.

Legalism, inherited from St. Augustine, distinguishes between *reatus poenae* (burden of punishment due to sin that needs "satisfaction," Augustine's main reason for the existence of purgatory) and *reatus culpae* (the guilt incurred but "absolved" through the sacrament of reconciliation).

Today, we find it much easier than at earlier times to consider the whole human person as continuing to exist after death with the same consciousness of personhood as he or she acquired in earthly life. Karl Rahner is representative of the new theologians, who see purgatory as a necessary therapy unto total integration and wholeness of body, soul and spirit relationships. It is seen as a further maturing of the individual after death and a firm rejection of a God who vindictively heaps punishments upon us for past sins. Rather, we become the source of our own punishment and frustrations of our potentialities because of our free choices that have caused disharmony in God's right order. This is the way Rahner describes the therapy of purgatory:

> . . . purgatory comes to mean, plausibly, that the soul, after surrendering her concrete bodily structure and, indeed, through that act of surrender, comes in her free, active and morally self-determining state, to experience acutely her own harmony or disharmony with the objectively right order of the world and even, by this fresh appreciation, to contribute positively to the establishment of that right order. (*On the Theology of Death*, p. 33)

We can easily understand that few human beings in their lifetime will have succeeded in their relationships to God, fellow human beings and the world around them, to have reached their full potential as human persons. From our own personal history, we see so often that inadequacies come from other outside forces influencing us. We may die opting for God, yet such a choice has not filtered into the unconscious where strata upon strata of human experiences have been stored up from our earthly life. These experiences have not been fully penetrated by divine life and have not been brought consciously into the life of the Risen Christ.

It will be difficult for us to imagine how this processs of further integration of divine life into the past experiences (and even new ones!) of our earthly life will take place. Yet this entire process of painful integration of the whole of our stratified being into a definitive surrender of ourselves totally to the loving will of God the Father continues as during our earthly existence under God's grace. God's grace, as in this life, so in therapy is necessary to move us into fully realized persons in God's love. The loving service of other creatures, angelic spirits and human persons, the saints, and our loved ones also living in the new existence and those loved ones still living on earth is also instrumental in our healing.

Jesus' View Of Death

Jesus saw His own earthly death as a part of greater human growth and a movement to a higher sharing in God's eternal life. What struggles and temptations to hold on to the control of His earthly life did He overcome to arrive at a state of complete abandonment to do only the Father's will by making the Father the center of all His strivings?

Through His resurrectional presence, and the outpouring of His Spirit, Jesus fulfills the purpose of His coming to earth. He came to bring us life that we might have it more abundantly (Jn 10:10). Jesus tells us in John's Gospel, "I am the resurrection and the life. If anyone believes in me, even though he dies, he will live, and whoever lives and believes in me, will never die. Do you believe this?" (Jn 11:25-26). The death and dying process He underwent all His earthly life, and that He insists we also embrace, is a going against any power, control, spirit of possessiveness and complacency in being our own "god."

He calls us to live each moment with God as the center in the daily experience of God's outpoured love in Him, Jesus, and His Spirit. Through such a transformative love, we are to fulfill the two commandments: love God with our whole heart and love our neighbor as ourselves. The Christian view of death comes out of faith in Jesus Christ Who, by dying for love of us and rising, might share His eternal life, the very life of the Trinity within us. He conquers all sin and death in us.

In dying to the old creation, which sin built up as illusory and opposed to God's true order, we live in a new reality. We enter into harmony between ourselves and God's triune community of love. We enter into communion with the angels and saints, with our loved ones living on this earth or departed into the life to come. We enter into a pan-cosmic oneness through loving service to build the Body of Christ out of this created universe.

A New Attitude Toward
Our Departed Loved Ones

This gives us, therefore, a changed attitude toward our departed loved ones. We all, as Christians, give an intellectual assent to the belief that our beloved ones do live immediately and, therefore, forever after their earthly death. But God wants us to *really* believe by responding in living faith that the deceased are truly alive, the same persons whom we have known and loved while they lived among us.

If all this is true, does it exercise an influence on our daily relationships with our departed loved ones? It is so easy to live without real faith in the fundamental teaching of God's revelation by consigning our departed ones to a "loss" since they are no longer among us. Then we feel our attachment toward them to consist of a sick longing to hold them in memory, as captives, in the way we would like to think of them, while ignoring the true way they now exist toward us and God and His world.

If we have a lively faith that the dead are still very much alive and that they have the same consciousness, same love relationships with us, same attitudes they had before dying, this should exercise great influence on our attitudes as we continue to relate even more dramatically and with greater love than in times past.

Do you find this a bit spooky? Is this a bit of spiritism,

an encouragement to make contact with the dead? Has this not been forbidden by the same Church that teaches us to have loving contact through prayers and sacrifices with the dead? Scripture is rather strongly against conjuring up the spirits of the dead. The example of King Saul visiting the necromancer (one who contacts the dead) of Endor, stands as typical of church rejection of spiritism that seeks to contact dead spirits to receive knowledge of the future or power from some diabolical force (1 S 28:3-25).

But God's revelation, through the Church's constant teaching and liturgical practices of praying for the dead, shows us that there can be a wholesome communication in loving service that takes away the sting and victory of death (1 Co 15:55).

A Greater Love Through A Deeper Faith

Thus we should learn to exercise our faith in the possibility of our coming into deeper communion with our departed loved ones and in our desire to bring healing love to them in their lack of complete integration. C. S. Lewis, in his classic on bereavement, *A Grief Observed*, shares with us a most important truth, which he arrived at through his anguish at the death of his wife. Through the application of his Christian faith, he came to realize in his grief that death allowed him to love, not only his wife, but also God in a deeper manner and with a purer motive, removed from any idol-casting of the one he loved in such a rich, though manipulative way.

He discovered that the more he forgot himself with all the "phantasmagoria" which he had created to keep his wife more dead and turned to God in humble faith, the more he came into a more real, loving communion with his wife. He writes:

> And suddenly, at the very moment when, so far, I mourned H. [his deceased wife] least, I remembered her best. Indeed, it was something (almost)

better than memory, an instantaneous, unanswerable impression. To say it was like a meeting would be going too far. Yet there was that in it which tempts one to use those words. It was as if the lifting of the sorrow removed a barrier. (p.54)

How Are We To Love Our Departed?

If we on this earth believe our deceased loved ones are very much alive, how can we make contact with them? We are not to fashion false idols of the one living God of Abraham and of Jesus Christ. But we are to approach them through exercised faith, reflecting on God's revelation, that we can be in communion with a living God. So also we are to exercise faith in God's revealed truths about the living presence of the departed and our ability to be in loving communion with them in order that they may reach greater eternal happiness.

We are to love them unceasingly and unselfishly in the love of God. We seek their presence, we pray for them by offering ourselves in loving service in the one Body with Christ, our Head, to do all we can to make them eternally happy.

We should strive to turn often, as we do toward God, so also to our dead loved ones, who perhaps in God's eyes are more "alive" than we are. It's not "weird" to speak to them just as we do speak lovingly to God, to angelic spirits and human saints in glory.

Living The Sacrifice Of Christ In The Mass

The greatest sign of our love for them is to celebrate the sacrifice and sacrament of love of Jesus on their behalf. This is not merely to have Masses offered for their "repose," expecting in a magical, mechanistic way that the departed will soon "pop" out of purgatory. It necessitates our living the

Mass by interceding for our loved ones with our personal love shown in our daily life of constant love, even to the point of giving our lives for our suffering loved ones.

The Church exhorts us to pray and offer sacrifices, especially the Divine Liturgy, for the departed. If we can intercede for each other on earth, praying over them for healing, how much more now that the physical world can no longer separate us from them? Yet, therapeutic healing cannot be administered solely to the sick, the fearful, the angry. We are tied by the cords of human love and, therefore, we mediate Christ the Head and His healing love by our very personal, historical love, which we bring in honesty and sincerity that our beloved ones may know their identity as beautiful in God's love through the sacrificial love we offer them. When we love one another, God's very own love is being perfected (1 Jn 4:12).

When I Was Sick, You Visited Me

We have the power, by being living members in the Body of Christ, to bring His healing power to those who are sick. Your loved ones in purgatory have need of you, who are bonded through so many shared experiences with them. In their new life, through the therapy that you can help them undergo, they can experience how God has incarnated His loving gift of self to them through the love of Jesus Christ, His mother, Mary, and the angels and saints, and—so humbling to you—through the particular love that you show them.

They will yearn in their hearts to stretch out toward you in order to complete these loving friendships and to receive healing for the lack of love in their lives through the fresh love they receive now from you. Yet, part of the therapy will be in their realization of the lack of love they showed you in the past, as well as their agonizing inability to love you as they ought.

They will understand, also, how indifferent they had

been, through prejudices, fears, ignorance and simple sinful selfishness, toward you and so many other persons sent into their lives to love or to help and from whom they turned away. Such a lack of unity in love will be painful and healing as they seek eagerly to make amends for any dissension they may have responsibly brought into the Body of Christ. This is why those in purgatory also have a power of healing love as they turn to make amends to you and others, both living and dead, to become a new channel of healing love.

Healing Power Of Loving Prayer

Now we can see why the Church has always encouraged the faithful on earth to offer prayers for the departed in the belief that such prayers from those on earth can benefit the departed in purgatory. But this necessitates going beyond mere recitation of prayers with one's "heart" accompanying such petitions for the departed in purgatory. Prayers become an expressed communication of love toward another, expressed to God on behalf of the one praying.

When you lift up your prayers, accompanied by great self-giving love in service for the happiness of the departed, such a departed loved one stretches out in her/his loneliness and self-centeredness, like a person in prison stretches through the barred windows to contact help outside, to be called into "being" by a loved one who recognizes and loves him. Love alone heals and breaks down the walls of terrifying loneliness and self-centeredness.

When the departed are remembered with deep love by you still on this earth, they are called out of the tomb of isolation into a newly-found state of self-identity. The healing power of love consists of the therapy of destroying isolation and building a community, a oneness, a togetherness in loving union, which is always in loving union with the triune, divine community of one and many.

When you love others and want to be present to them,

even though death may separate them from you, they can experience a true finding of themselves through your love for them. They experience an expansion of their self identity and a growth in complexity-consciousness. This we all experience in this earthly life. We feel our inward being has expanded, but we experience also an openness to the outside world, a sense of great solidarity that allows us to be of fulfilling service to others. In true, unselfish human love, we approach closest to timelessness to the eternal now of God's unselfish divine love.

We become aware of a new level of existence, still rooted in a material existence that transcends the temporal. How beautifully Blessed Robert Southwell, SJ, the 16th-century English martyr, expressed this truth in a poem: "Not where I breathe do I live, but where I love." We move into a consciousness that we feel could know no fatigue and no end of growth. True love, by its nature, is always creating within us a new capacity for greater love. At the same time, it means a new capacity of *being* to give ourselves to another, and a new capacity to receive *being* from the one loved. In a way, there cannot be heaven without purgatory, no resurrection without a dying to a lower level of holding onto our gift of life instead of giving it away in loving service to help others.

Becoming A Healer To The Departed

We have seen that the death of a loved one does not separate us from communion with Christ and with each other. And to the degree that there is a reciprocal faith and trust in Christ, the one Mediator and Healer for all broken human beings, to that degree can there be deep healings, not only of the departed, but also of those still living in loving relationships that may still be full of pain and suffering. We should never pity those who die believing that Christ is the true Savior Who, by His death and resurrection, brings eternal life to all, who open up to receive His gift. The communion we share with the saints and our own beloved departed

57

will always, even in the life to come, remain something beyond our own expectation and knowledge in its dimensions and depths.

The *Letter to the Hebrews* exhorts us to keep ever in mind the centrality of Christ and His power of intercession. "Let us not lose sight of Jesus, who leads us in our faith and brings it to perfection: for the sake of the joy which was still in the future, he endured the cross, disregarding the shamefulness of it, and from now on has taken his place at the right of God's throne" (Heb 12:2-3).

One thing that is important to keep in mind is that we are to avoid any striving for certain psychological and subjective feelings of encountering the departed one that might remove us from the area of centrality of faith in Christ, Who can, and does, truly work through members of His Body to bring about healing of those, both living and dead, who are in need of His saving graces. We pray for our departed and we ask their prayerful assistance to the degree that both of us are one in Christ. To seek any other affirmation of our oneness is to turn away from Christ as the Head of the Suffering Body.

C.S. Lewis gives us a good description of his encounter with his departed wife that should summarize and guide our meeting with our beloved departed and the possibility of ongoing communion with them:

> It was quite incredibly unemotional. Just the impression of her *mind* momentarily facing my own. Mind, not "soul," as we tend to think of a soul. Certainly the reverse of what is called "soulful." Not at all like a rapturous reunion of lovers. Much more like getting a telephone call or a wire from her [his deceased wife] about some practical arrangement. Not that there was any "message," just intelligence and attention. No sense of joy or sorrow. No love even, in our ordinary sense. No un-love. I had never in any mood imagined the dead as so—well, so business-like. Yet, there was

an extreme and cheerful intimacy. An intimacy that had not passed through the senses or the emotions at all. (*A Grief Observed,* p.54)

An area of great concern for Christians who lose loved ones through death, who may never have seriously "practiced" Christianity or have known much about the saving power of Jesus Christ, is whether Christians can help them in their new afterlife. This problem touches many of our human relationships, starting with aborted fetuses, miscarriages, stillborn babies, infants who die prematurely, retarded children, as well as adults, and the millions and millions who die without a living faith in Christ as the Savior of the world.

Various solutions over the centuries of Christianity have come forth from theologians, who have grappled with the mystery of salvation for those who physically, psychologically or spiritually have not matured enough, deliberately or indeliberately, as to die without faith in Christ. One attempt we must reject is that which arose in the early Church of the 3rd century with the name of *universalism.* This stems from zealous optimism that stresses complete faith in God's universal will to have all men and women saved. According to this false teaching, He, Who has this will and evidently has all power to accomplish it, will do so in the end, so that all human creatures will be saved and there will be no eternal hell. This would embrace all unbaptized babies, aborted fetuses, and "pagans" who never came to know the good news of Jesus. *Limbo* is the teaching, but never accepted as dogma, that children who have died without grace of Baptism would be assigned to a "place" called limbo where there would be a natural state of happiness, but such children would never be able to share the full joys of heaven with their parents and the saints.

Some Principles

Here are some important principles that we need to keep

59

in mind in dealing with the communion of the saved and those on earth with those who have died without full knowledge of Jesus Christ.

1. God is love and He has freely created all human beings, including children, even in the fetal stage, in order that they may all share in His eternal happiness, that they may come to know and love Him. This will-act of God transcends all time and space and mysteriously exceeds anything we might think He must do and how He must do it. Nevertheless, God in this present order of salvation works through His visible Church and the sacraments to mediate Himself as loving gift to all human beings. Therefore, He freely calls other human beings in Christ's Body, the Church, to aid in bringing others to Him through their prayerful intercession and loving service, while they are on this earth and also in the life to come.

2. We must hold that Jesus died on the cross to save all human beings, including children (and human fetuses), retarded children and adults and those who have, through no fault of their own, but through cultural upbringing, been closed to the full message of God in His Son, Jesus Christ.

3. God never vindictively punishes anyone for all eternity. It is we, who, by our own choice of selfishness instead of true love for others, bring about self-inflicted punishment. We die with the type of consciousness that we have formed in our earthly relationships toward God, others and ourselves. Thus, no one will be deprived of God who has not freely turned away from Him through sins personally committed.

4. We become who we are and we live by values taught us in a community or lack of such. God brings His healing power to the broken by means of healthy members within the Body of Christ. Christ for all eternity will continue to heal and preach the good news of salvation by sending those closest to Him in loving union to extend His healing presence through their own involving love for the poor and the maimed. If God's mercy is above all His works, we can never

limit His love nor the way He will extend His love directly or indirectly through the living members of Christ's Body.

Extending Christ's Healing Through Your Loving Service

Thus, you and I have been placed by God's providence in a time and place within the Body of Christ. We are the results of loving relationships that have brought His presence to us and have made it possible for us to accept His love through the love of others. To the degree that we are united with Christ, to that degree we will hunger and thirst with St. Paul to come to the aid of others who do not know eternal life, the love of the Father, Son and Holy Spirit for each individual person.

Mothers and fathers of aborted fetuses, of miscarriages, of stillborn babies, or those who have died before reaching sufficient development to know God through faith, hope and love, all of them and all of us who are related to such seeming "tragedies" have a responsibility in deep faith to be in communion with such human creatures and by our love shown them to be the occasion for their continued growth in greater knowledge and human perfection of God's beauty and goodness toward them.

How many of us in our own families know of loved ones who have seemingly turned away from their Christian faith and died without any seeming conversion back to that faith? We have all known other persons who have never really had the opportunity to embrace the fullness of God's revelation through the visible Church of Christ. Today we are in touch with billions of those who are born and die in other religions that faultily teach opposition to Christianity or who die without any religious upbringing at all. Here we must realize the responsibility to intercede for them now and in their life to come.

By child-like faith in God's revelation through the teachings of the Church, we can be the "contact" point for many needy persons who have died and yet are in great need to encounter the Good News that Jesus Christ is for them. According to our readiness to sacrifice our own human ways of thinking and picturing those who have died, we all can be the instruments for the departed to encounter God's healing love.

Missionaries Of Witness

What agony and struggle for the parents of aborted children to put aside their own self-absorption of fears and guilt and to begin really to believe they can be in loving, healing communion with their "children," as they surrender to God's merciful forgiveness! What an area of missionary activity to be in loving prayer and sacrifice for the billions of human beings who in their new existence are opened to be evangelized by loving persons.

By our living in deeper faith and love, our Christian lives of intercessory prayer become synonymous with evangelization, as well as martyrdom. One true index of how the love of God has been poured into our hearts through the Holy Spirit (Rm 5:5) is our readiness to sacrifice our limited ways of viewing ourselves in relationship to the departed. To live with a burning desire to do all "to lay down" our lives for love of them, even those brothers and sisters whom we have never known except in Christ and the universal love which the Holy Spirit gives us, is the measure of our union with Christ.

As we are truly in communion with Him, we ardently wish to live to build up His Body. We begin to experience that whatsoever we do to the sick, the hungry, the thirsty, those in prison, those dying (Mt 25), we really do to Christ. The sacrifice of oneself in place of others is at the heart of Christianity. We are "in Christ," as a branch is inserted into the life-giving vine and able to bring forth the fruit of loving others as Jesus loves us. As He died on the cross in imitation

62

of the self-emptying love of His Heavenly Father toward each of His children, so His Holy Spirit inspires His disciples that the only sign whereby people will recognize them as followers is by the love they have for one another, for all persons.

You Can Make A Difference

I like to think (and how this will be done remains a mystery for us who are still on this earth) that the mercy and love of God, Father, Son, and Holy Spirit, continually go out in uncreated energies of love toward every human and angelic being created by God for union in the Body of Christ. God's healing love surely never ceases to pursue His children, especially those who have the greatest need. If so many billions and billions of human beings have never known His immense love for mankind in Christ Jesus, so often through no fault of their own, does not God continue to bring His healing love to them through the announcing of the Good News by the healthy members of the Body of Christ?

Is it farfetched to believe that Jesus still walks among such broken ones on this earth and already in the life to come through your loving eyes, hands and lips since you have been privileged to know Jesus Christ as your personal Savior? I like to imagine that the quivering lips of frightened children, now living among the departed, will be soothed to a smile, hatred of killers and prejudices of non-Christians toward Christ and His followers will be dissolved by loving persons like you and me, if we are ready to do all to help others become fully realized, happy persons.

Someday in the life to come, you and I will experience that there never was in God's view any separation between those on earth and those in the future life. The separation will be along the lines of ignorance of God's immense, perfect love made manifest through Christ and revealed through His members of His Body, the Church, or those who have accepted God's revelation brought into actuality through the Incarnate Word, Jesus Christ, working in His living members. We will experience the joy that so many persons, now largely unknown to us, will bring to us when they meet and ask us: "But why were you so loving toward me whom you never personally knew? Who are you? What have I ever done for you that you should have thought of me and sacrificed yourself for my happiness?"

Then you and I and other faithful members of the Body of Christ will understand finally what we lived by faith from Christ's revelation: "I tell you solemnly, in so far as you did this to one of the least of these brothers of mine, you did it to me" (Mt 25:40). And the broken ones will experience Jesus touching them and bringing them into the fullness of life. Those who never knew Jesus Christ will be led to the Head through His members, as they joyfully confess for all eternity: "We never knew such love!"

The Departed Have Need Of Us To Love

There is a wholesome way of needing others to love. God Trinity, in perfect agapic-love of self-emptying for each person, has need of the "other" to love in the hiddenness and *kenotic*, self-giving love of the Holy Spirit. The more the triune love of God lives within us, the more we have "need" to share that love that transforms us into beautiful, self-giving persons to become a gift of loving service to others.

We have already stressed the power of the saints and angels in their self-giving service to others in the Body of Christ. It remains to be pointed out in this chapter on relationships between the living on earth and those departed how the departed in purgatory and those in heavenly glory need to stretch out in a similar way as we, the living, need to exercise love toward the departed in their needs.

The Church clearly teaches us that not only can we on earth help the departed by our prayers and sacrifices, but also they in the life to come can help us in our journey toward our final goal.

My dear mother and father and younger brother have

already gone ahead into eternal life. Yet, in the case of each death, I have come to a new way of being present and in loving communion with them in a way I never could have conceived of before their deaths. I have learned to open up in deep faith to receive their loving presence. I have felt their active love and experienced their intercessory power in ways that seem to be miraculous and, yet, are so much of a building on earlier earthly loving communion, but now so unlimited by any restrictions of matter, time, space or selfish manipulation.

They have become healed in the therapy of love shown by me and their other loved ones, both on earth and those still undergoing their own healings in their new existence. As our departed loved ones become healthy in the Body of Christ, they are free by the merits of Christ to help serve us in our many needs.

This is the healthy communion that we can have with our departed loved ones and they with us unto greater oneness in Christ and oneness in loving service for each other. Their love is shown, no doubt, toward their own loved ones, toward those who have provided them healing love and toward those who are in great need of God's love in their lives.

Although angels and saints, filled with God's presence and purified of all selfishness, have greater powers of intercession, persons in purgatory have a God-given loyalty toward their loved ones and toward those with whom they had lived and worked on earth. As they stretch out toward God in intense intercession for their loved ones and acquaintances, new levels of heroism and love are reached. The Body of Christ is becoming fulfilled as Christ, the Head, brings all back to the Father in completion of God's eternal plan of all things in Christ and Christ in all things.

Purgatory Already A Sharing In Heaven

In conclusion to this chapter on relationships between those still living on earth and those departed, especially those in need of continued healing in the state called purgatory, we can now see that purgatory should no longer be a terrifying place of penal punishment. We should no longer speak of the separation that places an infinite abyss between us living and those dead, for it is only lack of love that separates persons and destroys all communion.

Rather, purgatory should be seen as a "place" of interchange between those persons who are close to God and those in need of overcoming spiritual obstacles in order to be healed and brought into a greater unity of love between members and the Head of the Body of Christ. In turn, we have seen that as they are healed they become loving intercessors toward the needy on earth and toward those with them in purgatory who need their loving presence.

Purgatory is real. It is as real as all of us who, both in this life and in the life to come, have not yet surrendered every part of our being, every relationship that has made us who we are, to Jesus Christ. It is painful. It is joyful. It is learning the lesson we never fully master during this exile on earth: how to die to our isolation and self-centeredness by letting go of our own illusory control over ourselves, others, over God Himself. It is also learning how to accept the healing power of God's love that comes to us directly through the triune uncreated energies of God's love.

It is experiencing new levels of life in the Risen Savior. It is a vital part of Heaven already. It is the ante-chamber to fullness of happiness, but not quite fully experienced. It leads to greater oneness in Christ in Whom we all have been uniquely created as a manifestation of God's beauty and love to others. Our prayers for the departed and their prayers for us, including the powerful intercession of the angels and saints, are always seen as part of the powerful and only true intercession of Jesus Christ, and as part of God's plan. Christian love for each other on this earth knows no end of growth in the life to come and is always measured by not closing in upon oneself, but by becoming open to transmit God's love to all others by our personal loving service to them in need.

When we need to love others by self-sacrificing service to those in greater need than ourselves, then we bring the humble need of God to them so they, healed, can love others with God's very own need to be love to all His children.

Chapter Four

ANGELS: MESSENGERS OF GOD

In our modern world there seems to be a prevalent, over-weening curiosity as to whether God has made creatures other than us "earthlings." As Christians, we believe that God has called all of His children to come to know His infinite love for them and to return that love. Through scientific developments in outer space, especially by placing human persons on the moon, we wonder whether there exist non-human, but material, creatures on other planets.

If there exist creatures of higher intelligence in outer space, what would Christ mean to them? Did He die to "save" them, also? Did they know sin? Another great curiosity existing among many moderns is the world of "spirits." Spiritism, the "art" of making contact with spirits, either those of deceased human beings or of angelic spirits, both good, "angelic" spirits or evil, "demonic" spirits or *devils*, is of overweening interest to an ever-increasing number of persons today, especially in our Western technological countries.

Are there really "spirits," creatures superior to us human

beings, not possessing human, material bodies, but "pure" intellectual spirits? Do they influence us in any way? How can we know that they really exist?

This leads us easily to want to reexamine the traditional teaching of angels as found in Scripture and the teachings of the Church. Prevalent, however, today, in our excessive appreciation of science and its perceptual knowledge from sense observation is an understanding that the existence and functions of angels (and, therefore, fallen angels, devils!) is very "unscientific." To hold their existence as pure spirits for many "modern" persons is to accept a simplistic, nonscientific view of the world that would explain natural causes all too readily by angelic intermediaries that God uses to keep our universe "on schedule."

Faith In Angels

First, we as Christians must hold that it is not "unscientific" for human beings to believe in the existence of pure spirits, known in the Judeao-Christian tradition as *angels*. We know their existence and their functions only through God's revealed words in Holy Scripture and the teachings of the Church.

If there exist good and evil human persons, it is not unscientific to believe that among pure angelic spirits there are good and evil spirits. Science is unequipped to pass judgment on whether pure spirits exist and what is their nature. This can come only by faith through God's revelation.

We can only believe, as Christians must, that God freely created intelligent, pure spirits. They are by God's revelation superior to us human beings, but they are meant in God's decrees of creation to be a part of bringing His creation into His designated completion. Such a revelation of this knowledge, given us through Scripture and the affirmation of the Church's teachings throughout the centuries, should be considered as a gift-knowledge to help us human beings.

Throughout God's revelation in Scripture and the traditions of the teaching Church, we can accept on faith in God's revealed words a most important principle in God's relations to His created world. He uses creatures to give Himself, through revealed communications and by intimate, loving communion, to other creatures. God is love (1 Jn 4:8). Jesus Christ is the full revelation that God's love is constant, a concerned self-giving through a self-emptying love for His children. Integral to this belief is that God works through His secondary causes, especially those creatures given a share in His intellectual and volitional powers.

Thus, the Christian teaching, as enunciated so clearly by St. Paul, of the Mystical Body of Christ presents to us not merely other human beings but, also, angelic spirits as foci through whom God's uncreated energies of love, His personalized self-giving as individuated Father and Son and Holy Spirit, touch us and lead us into a sharing in their divine life.

Angels In The Old Testament

When we, therefore, approach this subject of angels as gifts to us of God's concerned and involved love, we see angels not as static natures but as pure spirits of highest created intellectual and volitional powers. Through their free choice to cooperate with God and other created agents, they serve this created world and help to bring it into completion according to God's designs.

As we turn to Scripture, we need to be aware of the literary nature of any given text of the Old or New Testament. Are we reading a text narrating the simple facts of history, or is it an embellished story-telling technique to exalt God's power working in our material world through popular views of the world with spirits active in each event?

The ancient view of the world and the manner in which God operates in creation through angelic spirits as found, especially in the Old Testament, needs "de-mythologizing" and purifying of notions which, today, are no longer plausible to a scientific world.

71

This has been the valuable contribution of the Church in its traditional teaching and its role of purifying by its theologians the extravagant details which are not an essential part of God's revelation. Nor are these details essential to the intrinsic nature of angels.

The general, primary meaning of *angel* (in Greek: *angelos*) refers to non-material created spirits who are used by God as His *messengers* to convey His communication to human beings. But this function of service leads us in Scripture to see that the chief reason for God's creation of angels is to glorify God. We can argue that, if God has created us human beings to share in His explosive love to become "participators" of God's very own nature (2 P 1:4), God also has created angelic spirits to enjoy a share in His beatitude and happiness.

This is what Isaiah, the prophet, saw in his vision of the six-winged Seraphim who surrounded the Heavenly Throne and constantly praised God: "Holy, holy, holy, is Yahweh Sabaoth, His glory fills the whole earth" (Is 6:3). Daniel hints, also, at the primary purpose of angels as worship and adoration before the awesome throne of Yahweh: "A thousand thousand waited on him, then a thousand times ten thousand before him" (Dn 7:10).

Yet, in their relationships to human beings and the material creation of the earth, angels in revelation have a special function. The Letter to the Hebrews passed on to us the succinct revelation of the Old Testament that angelic spirits have a continued function of service toward us human beings and our material world around us. "The truth is, they are all spirits whose work is service, sent to help those who will be the heirs of salvation" (Heb 1:14).

Capable Of Sinning

Although they are superior in intellectual gifts to us material beings, angels are capable of sinning and turning away from adoring and serving God. Called to return God's love with obedience and love, some angels did sin. We read in 2 P 2:4: "When angels sinned, God did not spare them: he sent them down to the underworld and consigned them to the dark underground caves to be held there till the day of Judgment."

The Letter of Jude also describes in Old Testament language the fall of some angels: "Next, let me remind you of the angels who had supreme authority, but did not keep it and left their appointed sphere" (Jude 6). The first encounter in the beginning of the Old Testament in the Book of Genesis is with a fallen spirit tempting the first woman and man to sin.

Yet, God called the good angels to cooperate in bringing about His intended purpose in creating the physical universe. The second mention of angels in Genesis is the description of their role in effecting God's punishment and purification of the sinful human race. *Cherubs* are posted in front of the garden of Eden with "the flame of a flashing sword, to guard the way to the tree of life" (Gn 3:24).

Helping Friends

It should be a graceful inspiration for us to believe that God gives us angelic spirits to protect and deliver us from physical, psychic and spiritual "forces" that might threaten our journey toward God. We see both in the Old and New Testaments that angels are bearers of divine messages to human beings on earth. They give us insights and knowledge of what needs to be done in a given circumstance. They protect and rescue us from imminent dangers.

God brought, through protective angels and the prophet Elisha, the deliverance of Israel from the Arameans by sending them an army of angels with chariots and horses to rout the enemy camp (2 K 6:17).

St. Paul assured the sailors in the boat carrying them to

Rome that faced imminent shipwreck that God sent him in the night an angel who promised them all safe landing:

> Last night there was standing beside me an angel of the God to whom I belong and whom I serve, and he said, "Do not be afraid, Paul. You are destined to appear before Caesar, and for this reason God grants you the safety of all who are sailing with you." (Ac 27:23-24)

Angels In The New Testament

The Letter to the Hebrews gives us a long list of men and women who exercised heroic faith in God's love and power. They were delivered from sickness, natural calamity, persecutors, accidents, and even imminent death. In the later period of the writing of the Old Testament books, especially those of the Septuagint written in Greek, e.g., Job, Daniel, Tobit, when through Greek influences the transcendence of God was heavily accentuated, angels began to appear more frequently to serve as God's intermediaries. In earlier books written in Hebrew, Yahweh directly was credited with His own actions toward human beings.

But in the New Testament writings, with the revelation of Jesus Christ as the God-Man, the appearances of angels are very much purified of extravagant language. A greater balance is attained as Jesus Christ is preached as the unique mediator between the Heavenly Father and ourselves.

> In other words, brothers, through the blood of Jesus, we have the right to enter the sanctuary by a new way, which he has opened for us, a living opening through the curtain, that is to say, his body. And we have the supreme high priest over all the house of God. So, as we go in, let us be sincere in heart and filled with faith, our minds sprinkled and free from any trace of bad conscience

and our bodies washed with pure water. (Heb 10:19-21)

Angels continue their primary function as God's messengers to human persons (cf. Mt 1:20; 2:13,19 Lk 1:11,26; 2:9; Ac 8:26; 10:3; 27:23). They appear in dreams to Joseph, the husband of Mary. They appear to persons fully awake in apparitions, appearing as embodied persons, as in the case of the white-robed angel who appeared at the emptied tomb of Jesus before the women (Mk 16:5; cf. Lk 24:4; Jn 20:12).

They appear in visions to human beings and instruct them (Ac 10:3). At times, they resemble young men in shining white robes (Mk 16:5; Mt 28:3; Lk 24:4; Jn 20:12; Ac 1:10; 10:30; Rv 16:6; 19:14). We are taught that there are very many angels: "Or do you think that I cannot appeal to my Father who would promptly send more than twelve legions of angels to my defense?" (Mt 26:53; cf. also Heb 12:22; Rv 5:11) They are spirits, not material beings (Heb 1:14; Rv 1:4). They have been created in Christ (Col 1:16). They have been reconciled with God through Christ's blood (Col 1:20).

Angels are classified into groups dependent on their functions and are given names inherited from the apocrypha writings of the late Jewish periods just before the dawn of Christianity, e.g., the Book of Henoch. St. Paul lists several of the angelic groups, dividing them according to their different levels of excellence and power in service to God and His created world. He writes: "In Him [Jesus Christ] were all things created in heaven and on earth, visible and invisible, whether *Thrones*, or *Dominations*, or *Principalities*, or *Powers*" (Col 1:16). He adds other names, in the Epistle to the Ephesians, where he tells us that Christ is raised "above all Principality, and Power, and *Virtue*, and Dominion, and every name that is named, not only in this world, but also in that which is to come" (Ep 1:21).

To these five names tradition adds the choirs of *angels*, who appear throughout the scriptures, that of *archangels*, which occur twice in the New Testament, together with the *Cherubim* with flaming sword to guard Paradise against fallen

75

mankind and appeared in Ezechiel's vision (Ez 1:14) like flashes of lightning, and the *Seraphim* (the name is from a Hebrew word meaning to burn or flame) who touched the mouth of Isaiah with a live coal (Is 6:6).

St. Thomas Aquinas, following Pseudo-Dionysius in his treatise on *The Celestial Hierarchy*, gives us an amazing theological speculation as to the difference of functions between one choir and another. What is important in our understanding of angels is not to see them separated from their function of service and not uselessly indulge in speculation of how many can dance on the point of a pin. Their ministry is one of love of God and Christ in the building up of the Body of Christ unto the fullness of God's glory.

Ministry Of Service

Their primary ministry, as has been pointed out, is to worship and praise God. But in their ministry of service to this created world, especially to us human beings, we see an extension of their service of worship and praise as they aid us through their intercessory prayer before the Throne of God. Here we should believe in this revelation and act upon it whenever we enter into prayer. We should easily unite our hearts with them, human saints in glory, as well as with all the choirs of angelic spirits who, day and night, glorify the triune God.

They minister to us by communicating to us God's will and by unveiling God's word to us. They protect us physically and spiritually from all dangers of body, soul and spirit. They strengthen and encourage us not to weaken in our efforts. We must believe that, although angels can commmunicate ideas to us and be present to protect us from any type of harm, they cannot force us against our free will to do what they may suggest. They are always subservient to God, Who wishes us always to remain free to accept His attractions in the many ways God communicates His loving designs, especially through angelic spirits.

Guardian Angels

Despite the traditional teaching that each human person has an individual guardian angel to aid him in his journey through life, this has never been defined as a matter of faith. If there is any basis found in Scripture for the doctrine of an individual "guardian" angel, such a belief is not so much a custodial function of permanence and always one angel per person, but rather as a sign of God's protective love showing itself by sending His angelic messenger to us on a special mission. This doctrine of an individual angel protecting us on the right hand of each Christian, while the devil or a fallen angel occupied the left, grew out of proportion in the Middle Ages. We need to come back to the element of truth that this teaching highlights, and that is that God is involved in protecting us in all physical, psychic and spiritual dangers and does this through the cooperation both of angelic spirits and the saints of our human race.

This doctrine of a guardian angel essentially affirms what God has so clearly revealed in Scripture, namely, that God has an absolute providential care over all of us, His human creatures, made according to His own image and likeness. This care He exerts in many ways, always independently and gratuitously. Such protection is beyond our own fidelity and transcends our own human weaknesses. The fact that we do sin and fail to acknowledge God's protective angels should not lessen our belief in this basic truth that God takes care of us.

Evil Spirits

God's revelation in Scripture reveals much to us about evil, but never gives a clear definition of this basic problem that has haunted men and women since their creation. God created us human beings basically good. All about our nature is good, at least potentially, and not debased or evil. This principle of God's creation holds in Scripture for angelic spirits. God created all of them as good, not evil. Evil is a turning away from the goodness locked within all of God's creation. This is possible in angelic spirits and human persons, both of whom have intellectual and volitional powers to freely love the God they can come to know intellectually as beautiful and the Source of all other limited beauty.

How can we explain how some angelic spirits turned away from God in sin? Theologians, following St. Thomas Aquinas, generally hold that angels in their natural sphere could not have any ignorance or weakness of mind. The knowledge known to them is true and they cannot err in this way. But just as we have been called by God to enter into communion with a higher order, God's triune community of love, so angelic spirits were called through obedience to move into an order attained through faith, hope and love. In this higher order refusal, ignorance and evil become possible.

This is how St. Thomas describes the sin of angels: "In this way did the angel sin, because he turned his free will to his own good without reference to the higher rule of divine will" (St. Thomas: *Summa*, Prima Pars, Q. 43; art. 1, ad 4).

Through revelation, therefore, we find evil already on this earth in the form of the disobedient angelic spirits who fell away from the will of God. The presence of evil spirits on earth in the days of man and woman's innocence will always remain an insoluble mystery. In the Church's blessings and exorcism, the Church teaches us that evil spirits abide in material things. To the Church, the presence of Jesus as Conqueror of all sin and death on earth through His resurrectional power has been given this extension of Christ's power to drive out the influence of evil spirits and consecrate and sanctify such matter unto God's original plan.

In an appendix, I will present more on *spiritism* and *occultism*. Suffice it to say here that Satan and his cohorts tempt us to sin, even though they cannot enter into us and force our wills to act contrary to our conscience. It is not always so clear whether it be actual devils who go about like roaring lions seeking to devour us, as taught in 1 Peter 5:8-9, or such forces which lie deeply within our "unspiritual self," as St. Paul teaches (Rm 7:14-17). It is not necessary to know whether evil comes from extrinsic evil spirits or the result of our own evil inheritance through birth and social upbringing. What is important is that it is always within our power with God's grace and the help of the good angelic spirits to resist such diabolic or divisive forces. St. Paul writes, "Give not place to the devil" (Eph 4:27).

To ignore this power of evil spirits is to ignore a force much more powerful for evil than the seductions of evil human beings. This is why St. Paul warns us, "Devils are rulers of the world of this darkness" (Eph 6:12).

Devotion To Angels

The theology of angels has been changing greatly from a medieval mental game of discovering all we human beings could know about these "objective" beings to a more scriptural presentation of angels. What is most important in regard to angels is the consistent Church doctrine that God ministers to us on earth and in the life to come through His saints and angels. Such "ministering spirits" (Heb 1:14) are found throughout Holy Scripture as the messengers of God or powers stemming from God. What is important is that they make God's goodness concrete, both in this life and in the life to come. Their manifold ministry to us is considered in Scripture and in the writings of the early Fathers as a protection against the dangers which evil powers place in the way of the faithful. As cities are protected by their walls against the attacks of enemies, so the Christian is protected by angelic spirits who lovingly service us, since they experience the outpoured love of the triune God making them into beautiful, self-sacrificing persons.

We are in need of a child-like openness to allow our Heavenly Father, through His two hands, Jesus Christ and His Holy Spirit, to touch us and bring us into a greater sharing in His very own divine life. How God effects His protective love in our regard will be up to Him as He freely selects to "enflesh" His loving power through His messengers, His angels, in ways only He can determine. It is for us to be alert and expectant of His inbreaking love. Scripture prepares us to be surprised at the suddenness of God's messengers entering into our lives to relay His communicating words, to strengthen us in our weaknesses and to protect us from overwhelming dangers.

I have always been impressed by the Old Testament story about the prophet Balaam and his braying donkey. Perhaps God smiles when He tells us this story as He hopes the point about our encountering Him in His angels will be understood. You remember the story, no doubt. Balak, the king of Moab, fearing the power of the Israelites, entreated the prophet Balaam to pray a curse over Israel. Instead, Balaam pronounced a blessing over God's chosen people. Balak summoned Balaam to come to him but Balaam, astride his she-donkey, could not force the animal to go forward.

We read: "and the angel of Yahweh took his stand on the road to bar his way. . . . Now the donkey saw the angel of Yahweh standing on the road, a sword in his hand" (Nu 22:22-23). The prophet saw no angel in his path, even though the animal saw him. He beat his animal mercilessly until God spoke through the donkey: "What have I done to you? Why beat me three times like this?" Then God opened Balaam's eyes and he also saw the angel of Yahweh standing on the road with drawn sword. Balaam bowed down prostrate on his face and confessed, "I have sinned. I did not know you were standing in my path" (Nu 22:34).

Angels Everywhere

Are we not a bit like Balaam? He failed to see the angel encountering him as God's messenger in his path, even though the donkey was able to see him. God wishes us to be open and ready to meet that "something other" that lies beyond our normal human reasoning. The Bible, both in the

80

Old and New Testaments, speaks about angels because God wishes to point us in the direction of something that lies beyond anything we could comprehend through our usual theological concepts or rituals of worship. This "beyondness" is the free, mysterious encounter between God and His individual children. God can never be limited in the "how" by any creature.

Angels In Human Form

We have seen in the earliest accounts in the Old Testament of angelic encounters with human beings, that angels were God's messengers who looked very much like "normal" beings. At first, the angels are not recognized as God's messengers. We see this in the account of Abraham with the three visitors at the oak of Mamre (Gn 18). Abraham saw them as three ordinary travelers. Excitedly, and with great loving hospitality, he prepared a sumptuous meal for them. After the meal, one of the travelers gives the message to Abraham that his wife, Sarah, would bear him a child.

This is the world of angels we need to enter. With Abraham we are not looking for superhuman, angelic messengers, but we are, childlike, always expecting God to speak His Word in every social encounter with other human beings. Didn't Jesus tell us He would be present in the times we encounter the sick, the hungry, the thirsty, the dying, the imprisoned and, whatsoever we would do to them, we would do to Him (Mt 25)?

In all such angelic encounters we see God's Spirit allowing the person to recognize by the departure of the "heavenly messenger" that God has sent His messenger to help His beloved children. The stories of Abraham (Gn 18), Gideon (Jg 6:11-24), Samson's parents (Jg 13:1-25), the two disciples on the road to Emmaus (Lk 24) all present us with what seemed to be a mere human encounter that brought recognition of the presence of God's angel, or of Christ risen in the "special" way of departure of the heavenly visitors. Eyes that at first were closed suddenly become opened at the moment of departure of the "messenger" of God. The recipients knew that they had encountered God in a special manner through the agency of a heavenly spirit.

The Gift Of Angels

Once we firmly believe that we have only one high priest and intercessor, Jesus Christ, we can be opened to communion with the angels and saints as helpers toward sanctity. In no way should we ever see them taking us away from Christ's unique mediation. Rather, we should see the angelic spirits and human saints as extensions of God's gift of the triune community.

St. Thomas Aquinas gives us the basic law of God's economy of salvation whereby He mediates the gift of Himself, even of Jesus Christ, to us through angels and saints who have become perfected in Jesus Christ. He writes:

> It is the law of God's government of the world that the infirm should be helped and brought back to God by creatures. It is consistent with this willed order of things that the saints have reached their Heavenly Fatherland, and who "knowing that while we are in the body, we are absent from the Lord" (2 Co 5:6) should make intercession for us that we may be brought back to the Lord. This is precisely what is happening when the saints (and angels) obtain the favors of divine Goodness for us. And since our return to God must be in proportion to the effusion of His benefits upon us, and these benefits come through the intercession of the saints, so it is necessary that we make use of the patronage of the saints (and angels). Therefore, we call them our advocates with God and, we pray to them, we acknowledge them as our mediators.

How consoling it should be for us to live in the presence

of God's loving angels and saints! We should lovingly accept the doctrine of the Church that God has created angelic spirits whom He uses as channels to order the course of His created world. Part of the work of such beautiful and exalted spirits is to use their higher powers of intellect and will, superior to ours, to help and protect us in order that we, too, may be led with them into the fullness of redemption and citizenship in the heavenly kingdom.

Angels, therefore, show their love for God through their service for other creatures, just as we are enjoined to show our love for God by serving other human beings. St. Augustine teaches that angels form the heavenly city of God and this segment of the holy city comes to the help of the other part that is still pilgrimaging below. Both parts one day will be united and even now are one in the bond of love (*Enchiridion*, 56).

As the angels ministered to Christ personally, so now they minister to Him in heaven. It is for those who deny the existence and the power of angels to prove that God cannot come through the ministry of angels. The teachings of the great writers of the Church hold out to us the help angels can give us as instructors who lead us on to perform good works and who intercede for us who are, somehow, placed in their charge. It is a gift from the teaching Church for us to believe that God's infinite power can unfold through His messengers, His angels, as they enter into our lives in loving service.

In our present world, in which we are faced with so many perplexing forces of evil that fill us with overwhelming fear and anxiety, belief in the ministering love of angels should not be a childish "cop-out" into a world of fairy spirits, but it should be a grace from God that strengthens us in our struggle against such evil. We can learn to call upon the angels for help and protection in all human situations, even those that seem most desperate and hopeless. We can learn to communicate with God's communicating love by walking daily in the presence of our special angelic spirits who bring to concrete focus our belief in God's ever-abiding and activating presence in all details of our lives.

For those who have become like little children, the childhood prayer "Angel of God, my guardian dear, to whom His love commits me here, ever this day be at my side, to light and guard, to rule and guide. Amen" will have great meaning and bring strength and help toward sanctity. For others, angels do not exist simply because they fail to see them. Yet, even for them, the angels are real because God is real and loves us actively and powerfully. Even when we do not believe in them, God continually ministers in loving service to all of us, His children, through His "ministering spirits."

Chapter Five

HOLY MARY, MOTHER OF GOD, PRAY FOR US, NOW . . .

There is an ancient Russian legend that runs thus: St. Andrew, the Apostle and patron of the Byzantine Greek and Slav Churches, hurried to heaven, released by his crucifixion from earthly toil and anguish. St. Paul would have called him "The fool for Christ," for he loved the cross of our Savior and His Mother who stood at the foot of the cross. Admitted to the gates of heaven, he began searching for his beautiful, heavenly Queen. "Where is she?" he asked his guide. "She's not here," replied the angelic tour master. "She is in the suffering world drying the tears of her weeping children."

Drying their tears, healing their hearts, folding the hands of her suffering children, loving them, searching for them, teaching them, reminding them, praying with them, and interceding for them in their needs—these are the ways of heaven's Queen on earth. This is the way her Son, Jesus, lived on this earth and the way she herself lived before she died. This is the way most Eastern Orthodox and Roman

85

Catholics picture Mary in glory, still interceding actively for us on earth.

"Come To Me"

He had said before He died that He would draw all men to Himself. "I shall return to take you with me, so that where I am you may be, too" (Jn 14:3). Of all the members of Christ's Body, who but Mary enjoys the highest glory and oneness with Jesus Christ? As Mary intimately shared in the life, suffering and death of her Son, so the Church believes she shares now in His glory (Rm 8:17). She had come to serve Him with the total surrender of herself. She also has come into glory with Him (Mt 25:34). Jesus is the "first fruits and, then, after the coming of Christ, those who belong to Him" (1 Co 15:23). Mary belongs most intimately to Jesus as mother to Son, as the living member of His Body closest in relation to Him, the Head.

Intercession Of Mary

Mary's glory, like that of Christ, is not a static enjoyment of a heavenly reward. Her glory consists in being present to Jesus Christ and, through Him, present to the heavenly Father by the overshadowing of the Holy Spirit. But being present in love to her Son is to have His very own mind. It is to receive His infinite, perfect gift of Himself, but it is also for Mary to want continually to surrender herself to loving service.

As Jesus is now interceding for us, so Mary is united with Him in seeking to help us. If Mary on earth lived only for Christ, how much more now does Mary want to bring all beings to Him? The Church teaches us that Mary and all the saints, who have died in the friendship of Christ, are now living in glory. It means that Mary is, therefore, living with full consciousness, memory and understanding of our needs.

She exercises acts of love and compassion toward all of us still in this earthly exile.

Can we believe that Mary, who loved Jesus Christ so ardently in her lifetime, does not now burn with love and zeal to share her Son with all of us? If St. Paul yearned with great zeal to become all things to all men and women in order to win them for Christ (1 Co 9:22), we can imagine without any exaggeration the interest and zeal of Mary in regard to all human beings. St. Paul felt a spiritual maternity toward those whom he formed. "I must go through the pain of giving birth to you all over again, until Christ is formed in you" (Ga 4:19). Mary, who in her earthly life gave birth to Christ, wants continually in her glory to form Christ in all the children He has given her.

Mary in the early Church is conceived of as a prototype of the Church, the collective Mother, the womb wherein all of us, redeemed children of the heavenly Father, are brought forth unto Christ's new life. We must center here in a special way on Mary as person, historically the mother of Jesus, and in glory now vitally concerned with and lovingly relating to us as individuals. We cannot, however, separate Mary's loving activity on our behalf from her total submission to Christ's unique intercession.

Communion Of Saints

We have already seen that the Church has always taught doctrinally and devotionally that with the saints there is communication between the living in this life and those living in Christ in the life after death. Vatican II's Constitution on the Church reiterates this constant tradition: "The Church, too, has devoutly implored aid of their intercession."[1] We implore their intercession because we believe they

---

[1] *Lumen Gentium*, 50.

are, after death, even more alive and more loving, hence, more desirous to help us than when they lived their earthly life.

Among all Christians departed into life eternal, Mary is the most "possessed" by God's Spirit of love. She is "higher in honor than the Cherubim and more glorious beyond compare than the Seraphim," as the Byzantine Liturgy of St. John Chrysostom hymns her. She is more present to all of us than our most beloved parents, husband or wife, relatives or friends departed.

She is present to us by the immense "oneness" that she enjoys with the "oneness" of the Trinity. The prayer of Jesus to His Father in the Last Supper Discourse was fulfilled for His Mother, at least.

> Father, may they be one in us,
> As you are in me and I am in you . . .
> with me in them and you in me,
> may they be so completely one. . . .
> I want those you have given me
> to be with me where I am
> so that they may always see the glory
> you have given me. (Jn 17:21-24)

But Mary is also present universally to every human being by her activating love that seeks to serve the neediest of the children whom she ardently wishes to bring forth into God's life. Love of God in Mary is the uncreated energy of God seeking to become realized love through the humble service of Mary. At the heart of Mary's love and our love is a desire to share abundantly of the goodness God has given to us with others who do not have what we have.

The greater the gifts of love we receive, the more we have to share with others. Upon entering into her glory in heaven, Mary was full of grace. She was already declared full of grace by the Angel Gabriel when the Holy Spirit overshadowed her and she surrendered completely to serve her Lord in her humble lowliness (Lk 1:38). Yet, she grew in love of God as she allowed God's love in her to make her more open, more present, more serving to all who needed her. How she must have grown in grace as she served her Son, Jesus of Nazareth, for 30 years. How that grace must have reached a fullness at the foot of the cross that pained her to want to be present to each person in order that the blood of her Son might not be poured out in vain.

Growth In Grace

Now after 2,000 years of serving the universe from her state of glory, she has grown in greater grace, in greater love-presence of "God-in-her" toward the whole world. In a way, Mary needs us, all of us. Like a mother who needs a sick or retarded child to allow her the occasion and the conflict necessary for her to grow in greater self-giving love, so Mary needs the sinful and ignorant who live in darkness and absence of her Son. She lovingly intercedes for them as only a suffering mother can: "Father, forgive them, they do not know what they are doing" (Lk 23:34). She needs also the advanced contemplative to share her contemplative riches. The simple, ordinary Christian calls out a unique form of Mary's service as she seeks to urge him/her to greater generosity and intimacy with her Son. Thus, Mary grows in greater love by exercising a loving service to her children.

Mary in glory is constantly concerned with God's children. Beginning in her earthly life, Mary progressively grew in greater understanding of her motherly concern for all human beings. God infused into her, both in her earthly life and in her present glorified existence, a greater knowledge of the needs of all human beings individually and gave her a love that could take each person as her child and minister healing power as to her own Son.

Mary sees us all in God and loves us with the love that Jesus has for us. Through God's grace, she is so completely able to be at one with her Son that His understanding and love for us become also hers. She sees in each of us a part of herself because she sees us as a part, actually or potentially, of His Mystical Body. She wants only what Jesus wants for us. Her intercession, therefore, far from being separated from that of her Son, is one with His. As His intercession before His Father's throne is omnipotent, so Mary's intercession, one with Christ's, approaches to that degree, omnipotence. Her intercession is not of her own. It is of a similar nature as her words to the servants at the wedding feast of Cana: "Do whatever he tells you" (Jn 2:5).

Mary Compassionate

If Mary is in touch with all human beings and sensitive to their needs, how can we reconcile her being in the state of glory and still suffering with us? How do our sin and tepidity affect her in glory? Mary has brought into glory not only her body, but also all of her experiences in human living. She can now relive her suffering moments by relating them to different events and persons from the initial experience.

As she has been in intimate and involving concern with human beings for more than 2,000 years, she has been in touch with each period of Christian history in general and with the specific history of each person she has sought to help. Such active concern brings her to this present moment, allowing her to be compassionate and suffer when we fail to live as we ought. Our sinfulness must cause her sorrow, just as our cooperation with grace must add to her joy in heaven.

Apparitions Of Mary

This might aid us in understanding how Mary can externalize her invisible presence and manifest a state of sorrow at the failings of God's children. Apparitions of Mary to individual Christians throughout the centuries can legitimately have a prophetic or charismatic role to play within the Church. We must always distinguish between public and private revelations. Anything touching upon essential doctrines and moral values comes under the competence and duty of the hierarchical magisterium in the Church. Apparitions of Mary or even of Christ or saints and angels to individuals are peripheral to elements essential to human salvation and, therefore, are secondary. This is not to say such are not helpful.

Apparitions can call individual Christians who receive them or others who heed the messages given in such visions to a very concrete way of understanding important elements already clearly revealed and taught as a part of the Church's public revelation received from Christ and His Apostles. Mary's appearances at Lourdes, LaSalette, or Fatima show her concern for her children in a given part of the world at a specific time in history.

E. Schillebeeckx gives us important norms to situate Marian apparitions within the larger context of God's salvation in history.[2]

1. Such extraordinary, charismatic elements must be subordinate to the normal moral and religious life of grace informed by dogma. Such apparitions are never sources of new doctrines, but their messages can stir people to new fervor and a return to the Church's traditional teachings and sacramental means of sanctification.

2. We do not have to accept apparitions with any divine faith since they are always secondary to the supernatural, revealed truths. It is always a question of our natural acceptance or rejection of them.

3. When the Church gives any approbation, this must not be construed as an infallible proof for the historical truth and authenticity of the apparition in question. No one is obliged to accept such authenticity.

4. The Church may bless shrines, establish liturgical feasts and popular devotions but, again, such approbation does not pass any judgment on the historical authenticity.

---

[2] E. Schillebeeckx, OP, *Mary Mother of the Redemption* (N.Y.: Sheed & Ward, 1964), pp 146-162.

Mary's Concern For Us

We can imagine Mary, the mother of Jesus Christ and of His many brothers and sisters, being especially concerned with the billions and billions of people who, through no fault of their own, never came to know that her Son is the Savior sent to enlighten the hearts of all mankind. God can touch their lives in any way He wishes, but He has worked through the community called the Church. This Church owes its existence to Mary's first mothering of Jesus, her Son. God uses His new creation, the society of His chosen people, whose mother is Mary, to touch unbelievers. As we have been helped through the prayerful intercession of holy persons and their personal example, so we can believe that the saints, especially Mary, will be used by God as channels of His healing for those who have not met Jesus Christ as their personal Lord and Savior.

It is this powerful intercession in heaven of the saints that St. John writes about:

> A large quantity of incense was given to the angel to offer with the prayers of all the saints on the golden altar that stood in front of the throne, and so from the angel's hand the smoke of the incense went up in the presence of God and with it the prayers of the saints (Rv 8:3-4).

A Loving, Active Presence

Mary and the saints are living members of Christ's Mystical Body. Love of God and neighbor never comes to an end (1 Co 13:8). We can never imagine that Mary and the other living members of Christ are "up there" in heaven separated from us. They are where Christ is and Christ is present on earth, growing in His members. His Body is growing both in Heaven and on earth. St. Paul understood well this interaction between the healthy members and the injured or needy members: "If one part is hurt, all parts are hurt with it. If one part is given special honor, all parts enjoy it" (1 Co 12:26).

Mary is truly in touch with us and eager to do all in order that Jesus become Lord and Master in our lives. "For he must be king until he has put all his enemies under his feet and the last of the enemies to be destroyed is death, for everything is to be put under his feet" (1 Co 15:26). Our lives will change, if we can live in the active faith that assures us that Mary, the saints and all of our departed loved ones are in intimate communication with us. The more we are united consciously to Christ, the more we are united to His living members. The closer the saints are united with the Head, Jesus Christ, the more they desire to help us.

And Mary is the one human being who is the closest member to Christ in His Body. True love of Christ's Spirit in her is constantly transforming her into an active, loving Mother of us individually. Many of us have had a childhood devotion to Mary that made her very present to us. Becoming religiously "educated," we lose this living, childlike relationship. We have all too often relegated our devotion to Mary, as in reciting the Rosary, to a moralistic meditation on her earthly existence in order to find an extrinsic model upon which to pattern our concrete living. Cannot our devotion to Mary only too often be satirized as "See Mary, see Mary run, run like Mary"? We were taught never to do anything at a dance or on a date that Mary would not have done! That we have lost such a devotion can only be unto God's glory!

A New Devotion To Mary

We express our devotion to Mary always in language that comes out of a definite culture. Today, we are completely turned off in reading some of the expressions of St. Louis Grignon de Montfort, such as "becoming Mary's slaves." He, no doubt, had a tremendous love for Mary and expressed that devotion in terms that were meaningful for him and his contemporaries of times past.

93

We have had to stand back in our devotion to Mary to examine what is essential from what is cultural, accidental and, perhaps, in need of change. Both through a biblical revival and scholarly patristic research, we have been brought to a new awareness of what is essential in true Christian devotion to Mary. Our insights through in-depth psychology and sociology allow us to be more open to experience Mary as an archetype of what the Church is called to be and what we, as individual Christians, have been destined in our Baptism to become.

Yet, precisely because Mary is an historical person who lived as recorded in the Gospel as the mother of Jesus and who, the Church proclaims throughout 2,000 years of belief, is glorified in body and soul, a sign of what awaits us, she is not only our archetype, but she continues to be our heavenly Mother.

It is only the Holy Spirit that Jesus releases from the depths of our hearts Who can lead us into the presence of Mary as our heavenly Mother. He can give us a true and growing experience of her loving care for us without taking away from the centrality of Jesus Christ's mediation. On the contrary, the Spirit teaches us that Mary's sanctity is the gift of God's grace that has ever rendered her the lowly handmaid seeking only to exalt her Lord and Savior. She is completely dependent on God's Word. She defines her greatness and her relationship to us solely in terms of loving service to Jesus Christ.

That same Spirit gives her and us the intuitive knowledge that she is always the Mother of God, full of grace, seeking through her powerful union with her Son to bring us forth as loving children through His Holy Spirit.

Mary Not The Church

Because Mary is an individual person and not a mere type of the Church collectively, we can be devoted to her, person to person, in a way that we cannot be devoted to

Mother Church. The Church is, like Mary, a virgin and a mother. Yet, it enjoys a mission of teaching, sanctifying, and administering through the extension of Christ's mission on this earth in time.

In this teaching, sacramental and pastoral ministry, Mary has not been confided a direct role. Through the Church, Christ lives and acts in space and time on this earth. Mary, while on earth, was not given a part in the Church's teaching, sacramental worship and priestly hierarchy.

Yet, these functions of the Church, if they are to bring forth Christ's life effectively into our world today, must be rooted in grace, love and prayer. The Church is first Mary, feminine, contemplative, completely surrendered to the overshadowing of the Holy Spirit. Out of His obedient submission, the Church takes on the masculinity of Jesus Christ, who ministered to the poor and the sick, the possessed and the sinful.

But we who are the Church become one with Mary in our devotion to her in our life of prayer. Without deep prayer, we will always look upon Mary as an object, someone who, aggressively, in a powerful way, obtains things for us. Such devotion will always be a mockery and an offense to the Holy Spirit and to the Blessed Mother Mary.

But as we stand before her icons and statues in our homes, churches or wayside chapels, the Holy Spirit will render us one with Mary. We will become devoted to her not by imitating her *actions*, but by becoming what she is: the Virgin Mother of God.

A few years ago, I was able to spend a semester at Tantur, the ecumenical institute for advanced theological research. It is located outside of Jerusalem on a knoll overlooking the fields of Bethlehem. The town of Bethlehem is about two miles away so, often, I enjoyed walking through the fields on its outskirts. The hills are dotted by numerous caves. My favorite occupation on such walks was to enter into these caves and go through a meditation.

I would begin by imagining St. Joseph taking Mary down

from the donkey after their fatiguing journey. He enters the cave and leads Mary inside. As he places the lantern on a rock, Mary's eyes adjust to the dimness around her. There is dankness, a wetness that makes it a bit difficult to breathe. She sees the mildewed straw, bugs and insects scurrying about; the animals stand mute in their caked dung. Cobwebs hang menacingly from the ceiling and walls. And, then, I always hear her say, as she looks upwards, "God, you have *got* to be kidding! Do you really want me to bring forth Your Son in this cave?" And God comes back with a sense of humor that only He can afford to entertain in such circumstances, "Yes, Mary, right on! Right on this dirty, stinky straw!"

My Lord and my God! I fade into the background with the shepherds and the animals. Mary has brought forth God and laid Him in the manger. The cave is transformed into the most beautiful cathedral! It isn't architecture that makes the temple of God, but *presence*! She has brought forth the presence of God into this broken segment of our world. The Body of Christ begins to grow and Mary is His Mother.

Mary is still that mediating presence of God in the caves of our hearts, in our broken, dark selves. It is His presence that can transform our caves into beautiful temples of God. But Mary is always there asking her Lord, "Do you really want me to bring forth Your Son in this cave?"

It's only a meditation, yet, somehow, it makes Mary seem more really the Mother of my Lord. I don't understand all the theological distinctions of her causality. All I know is that she is God's Mother and God continues to want her to bring Jesus Christ forth within me, in my daily life. I know, also, she is my mother and I love her for the great love she has for me. I always leave the Bethlehem cave knowing that God is a presence of love that can transform the dank darkness in my heart into the warmth and light of the Spirit of Jesus. And I know, also, that Mary is a similar presence of love, as she lovingly mediates the presence of her Son for me in my life.

As we pray, "Holy Mary, Mother of God, pray for us *now*

. . . ," we will experience her loving, motherly presence. She will become the channel of grace that will make us true members of the Church, of Christ's Body. We will live constantly in her holy presence, trusting that she who is all powerful before her Son will intercede for us, not to obtain so much this or that favor, but more importantly, that we become like her, a living oneness with Jesus Christ. We pray and live the prayer of St. Paul that Mary our Mother is always offering to her Son through His Holy Spirit:

> All I want is to know Christ and the power of his resurrection and to share his sufferings by reproducing the patterns of his death. (Ph 3:10)

Chapter Six

BE INTERCESSORS

When we repeat the creedal phrase "I believe in the communion of saints," what usually comes to our mind is the restrictive sense of the powerful intercession of the great saints in glory on our behalf, still living on this earth, and for those in purgatory. We so easily separate, as has already been pointed out, the "parts" of the one Body of Christ. The saints and good angels make up the Church Triumphant. The Church Suffering are those being purified in purgatory before they can advance into full, eternal life. And then we Christians of the Church Militant, still living on this earth, are trying to engage in the spiritual battles that will allow us to "take" heaven by violence.

This chapter, therefore, will focus exclusively on the intercessory role Jesus Christ and His Spirit call us to embrace within the Church, Christ's Body.

For most Christians there exists a confused understanding of petitional and intercessory prayer. In all the Christian liturgies there are places found for petitions by individuals of the worshipping community, as well as those general petitions offered by the presiding priest or minister. Yet, many Christians, through a better biblical understanding of intercessory prayer, take on the great responsibility of doing more than merely offering God petitions for their own needs and the needs of others.

A Real Difference

This is the real difference between petitional prayer and that of intercession. The petitioner, so to speak, "stays out of it," is asking God to do something for nothing, presents Christ's merits (for has He not done it all?), but personally does not obey Jesus' command to love others as He loves us. The intercessor is moved by a oneness with the Spirit of the Risen Jesus to become the go-between with God and the sinner or person(s) in need.

The intercessor, moved by the experienced indwelling presence of Jesus crucified, desires ardently to enflesh His love for the sinner, ready even to lay down his life for the needy. The intercessor is totally involved in wanting to do all with Christ and His Spirit to combat evil and sinfulness. Such a Christian wants to break down any wall that divides God from His children. He knows, unlike the petitioner, that true intercession demands sacrifice.

Jesus Christ, The Only Redeemer

Sharing in Christ's intercessory power does not take away from Christ's power to be the sole intercessor unto salvation. It is important now to show that the unique intercession of Jesus for all creatures, including angels, allows us to become true intercessors when we put on His mind and ask, as He promised us, in His name.

One of the most heart-gnawing experiences common to all human beings is that of loneliness. We all know what it means to feel isolated from everyone. There seems at times to be no one who understands us, no one to smile at us, give us a pat on the back, look lovingly into our eyes and assure us of their unselfish love and devotion. When we project this feeling of loneliness and estrangement to the whole human race, we begin to understand a bit better what it meant in God's design that Jesus Christ, the Word of God made flesh out of love for us, should empty Himself of all dignity to take upon Himself the form of a servant (Ph 2:6-7) to win our trust.

> He was wounded for our transgressions. He was bruised for our iniquities. The chastisement of our peace was upon him and with his stripes we are healed. (Is 53:5)

He Became Sin For Our Sakes

He became sin for our sakes that we might be delivered from sin. St. Peter powerfully describes Christ's infinite love for mankind: "Who in his own self bore our sins in his own body on the tree that we, being dead to sins, should live unto righteousness, by whose stripes you were healed" (1 P 2:24). Jesus Christ, being God, always merited to stand before His heavenly Father, to intercede with Him for the whole world with infinite dignity and power. Yet, His mediation for mankind had to be first a winning of man's trust in Him. He was by nature the mediator of the Father. All things were created in and through Him.

Yet, to qualify to become the mediator of mankind, to be the spanning bridge into humanity, He had to dip into the other side, to be rooted in the bank of humanity as He was from all eternity by nature rooted in the bank of divinity. Our human alienation from God through sin caused an abyss of loneliness within the human heart that could not be alleviated except by an experience of love at first hand. In the fullness of time, God became man, "the Word became flesh and dwelt among us" (Jn 1:14). "For God sent not his Son into the world to condemn the world, but that the world through him might be saved" (Jn 3:17).

The beginning of redemption is the moving out of my

loneliness by an experience that God really loves me to the folly of the cross and that, as St. Paul would say so often, "For me he died!" (Ga 2:20). Jesus Christ, therefore, becomes the greatest of all prophets because He literally stands between God and us and through the love of His Holy Spirit He goes to the Father in perfect, self-surrendering love while, at the same time, He goes toward each human being in that same perfect, self-giving love. Jesus Christ, therefore, mediates us to God, not so much by words said, but by a presence of self-surrendering love.

The human intercessor today is primarily this type of mediator. We know that there is only one, unique Mediator and that is Jesus Christ. He has replaced all other mediators such as Moses and the early prophets, all other sacrifices of the Temple unto blood of animals. He is the Mediator Who can reconcile the two separated parties, God and the human race, because He belongs to both worlds. He is God and Man. He is the only ultimate High Priest because He, the Offerer, is also the Gift offered. He is the Priest and the gift offered at the same time.

> And for this cause he is the mediator of the New Testament, that by means of death, for the redemption of the transgressions that were under the first Testament, they who are called might receive the promise of eternal inheritance. (Heb 9:15)

The Christian Intercessor

Yet, the Christian intercessor, by participating through the power of the Holy Spirit as intimately as possible with the sufferings of the human race, its sinfulness and alienation from God, seeks also by deep, prayerful union to abide in Jesus Christ, and through His powerful intercession to beg the Father for forgiveness and reconciliation. The prophet Jeremiah is a very special model of human intercessors. No other prophet shows such intense feeling and compassion for the fate of his people. He associates with their infidelity, pleads before God with confidence, is torn asunder by their coldness and rejection of him and of God's covenant.

Jeremiah becomes a model of Jesus Christ and of the modern Christian through mediating God's message of conversion by his own example. We know how the kings had been chosen by God as mediators of His people. The king of Israel, through his anointing, became officially the representative of his people, the one to speak to Yahweh on behalf of the Chosen People. He rendered thanks to God for his people. He spoke lamentations in times of national crises. As he functioned on behalf of God's People, he was obligated to function as God by ruling the people with justice.

The prophets from the 8th century B.C. on replaced the kings and they mediated God's mercy toward a people that was turning away from God. Jeremiah brings in his own life the fullness of prophetic mediation as he becomes a model of what Jesus Christ would be toward God's new people. Jeremiah pleads with God even though he feels it is hopeless. He, the intercessor, the mediator, and his people become one and the same person. Yet he is also one with Yahweh. He understands why God should not renew His covenant with them. "You walk, everyone of you, in the hardness of your evil heart" (Jr 16:12). His heart is torn by his people's coldness to Yahweh. "Cleanse your heart of evil, O Jerusalem, that you may be saved" (Jr 4:14). Yet he stands with boldness before Yahweh, never forgetting his people. He is aware of being called by God, even from the womb to be dedicated to this mission of mediation of God and His people. Though he would like to run away from his calling, yet he continues in faith to stand before Yahweh and intercede.

And God heaps upon Jeremiah, as upon a microcosm of Israel, His wrath to the point of breaking him. Yet, in faith he mediates his people by being totally obedient to Yahweh. God has His complete way with Jeremiah until Jeremiah is cut off completely from his people, rejected, alone. "Know that for thy sake I have suffered rebuke. . . . I sat not in the assembly of the mockers, nor rejoiced. I sat alone because of thy hand, for thou has filled me with indignation" (Jr 15:15-17).

Alone Before God

You, as intercessor, are called to "aloneness," to stand between God and your people. Out of your great love for your people that has forgotten God, you share in their alienation from God. Although you love God and seek at each moment to do God's will, yet your love for your fellow human beings becomes so great that you associate their sins with your own, as though you were the guilty one. With Moses you stand before the face of God and pray boldly that, if God does not forgive the sin of your people, "blot me, I pray thee, out of thy book which thou has written" (Ex 32:32).

Love Of Neighbor

So great is the love of the modern intercessor for his people that he pleads in prayer that God may grant him to suffer for their punishment. St. Symeon the New Theologian (+1022) grasped the role of prophet as mediator and intercessor for his people in writing the following words:

> ... he would wish with such zeal the salvation of his brothers, that often he would beg God, the Lover of men, with all his soul, with burning tears either to save them with him or to condemn him with them, refusing absolutely to be saved alone and in this imitating the attitude of God and that of Moses. So greatly tied spiritually to them by holy charity in the Holy Spirit, he would not even wish to enter into the Kingdom of Heaven if he had to be separated from them.

Like Jesus Christ, you, as intercessor, live in two regions: you live totally among other human persons, feeling every tear, every suffering and anguish of your brother or sister as

104

your own. Yet you move through life as though you were already in the presence of your heavenly Father. You experience daily that you are already a child of God and co-heir with Jesus Christ of heaven forever (Rm 8:17).

You, as intercessor, act much as a chemical catalyst. You begin a process of internal action, of conversion of the heart. For this you must be completely within the process. Yet, you must not become immersed in the process so that you are swept into the process that goes on in another's soul. We read, "And *almost* all things are by the law purged with blood, and without shedding of blood there is no remission" (Heb 9:22). There is a perfecting, a cleansing that comes by ministering the word of God. It is the perfecting of the saints to render themselves supple instruments under the Holy Spirit to become true mediators through whom the Word of God may be communicated to others.

God puts His hand on the intercessor called to mediate the Word. He cleanses His chosen instrument, not only in body, but in soul and spirit. Every thought is placed under God's scrutiny. It is God's living Word within you that cleanses you.

> Having therefore, brethren, boldness to enter into the holiest by the blood of Jesus, by a new and living way, which he has consecrated for us through the veil, that is to say, his flesh, and having a high priest over the house of God, let us draw near with a true heart in full assurance of faith, having our hearts sprinkled from an evil conscience and our bodies washed with pure water. (Heb 10:19-20)

This cleansing, pure water is the Word of God. Can you mediate God's word before you have been completely "washed" in it? The Word washes out of you all that is false doctrine, all that comes from yourself and is not of God's Word. It is losing your own identity by putting on the mind of Jesus Christ in all things. "If you continue in my word, then are you my disciples indeed. And you shall know the truth and the truth shall make you free" (Jn 8:31-32). To remain in Christ, the Word, you must be listening to His voice.

To become a mediator, you must have an open mind to learn more and more about the riches of that Divine Word. Remaining in that Word means constantly to study and think and pray about what the Divine Word has said in Scripture and is saying in your own life today. Your response is complete obedience to that Word, to all His commandments. You contemplate the Word and it leads you to action. The greatest function of mediating the Word is to mirror the Word completely in your own life as though your life were to be a lived Gospel story told in modern terms understandable by your contemporaries. Thus, you mediate the Word of God by being completely under the Word at all times in all your thoughts, words and actions.

A Special Call To Be An Intercessor

Jesus Christ, we have seen, is the only true Mediator, Who can adequately stand between the awesome holiness of His Father and the dark and evil sinfulness of humanity. Yet He calls all of us, His followers, to believe that He needs us to extend His intercessory presence into a certain time and place of this world. He, by giving us the gift of Baptism, has already enfolded us into Him and, therefore, into His intercessory power.

Salvation is a pure gift from God, not anything we have done (Eph 2:8-9). "We are God's work of art, created in Christ Jesus to live the good life as from the beginning He had meant us to live it" (Eph 2:10). He calls us to abide in Him and through His Spirit's life flowing with us, we, as branches, are to extend His reconciling love outward to the world (Jn 15:5-17).

He asks us to be fellow-intercessors with Him before the heavenly Father on behalf of the entire world that is groaning together in travail (Rm 8:22), to be brought out of death into a new creation. Are you your brother's and sister's keeper? Yes, your very concern to love actively every human

106

being demands that you join Jesus Christ in becoming His mediating presence of love, which reflects to an unloving world that our Father truly loves us.

As we look around our world today, we are overwhelmed by the forces of evil and ungodliness that seemingly increase daily over the weakening moral forces of loving unity. Selfishness of individuals, as well as of nations, shows the lack of sacrifice for the well-being of others. We wonder how long will God's patience be tested by His sinful children? Are we much different today than those in the time of the prophet Ezechiel?

> The people of the country have taken to extortion and banditry; they have oppressed the poor and needy and ill-treated the settler for no reason. I have been looking for someone among them to build a wall and man the breach in front of me, to defend the country and prevent me from destroying it, but I have not found anyone. Hence, I have discharged my anger on them; I have destroyed them in the fire of my fury. I have made their conduct recoil on their own heads. It is the Lord Yahweh who speaks. (Ez 22:29-31)

We have stressed that Jesus Christ, by His very nature as God-Man alone, is *the* Mediator, Who brings us redemption and reconciliation of the sinful to God. Now we need to see how we can, through the sanctifying work of the Holy Spirit, be sharers and extenders of Jesus' intercessory powers before the Father.

The Holy Spirit As Intercessor

If the Holy Spirit makes us into sharers of Jesus' intercessory power, it is because God's Spirit is also an intercessor. His intercessory power is different from that of Jesus Christ. The Spirit is the personified love uniting the Father and the Son within the Trinity. His role is always a mediational relationship of love. Love operates always in freedom of choice to accept love and to return it.

The same Holy Spirit operates, therefore, in filling us with His gifts of faith, hope and love and, thus, He enables us to be moved to the maximum of love for others as Jesus has loved us. He has loved us with such a depth of caring love that He laid down His life for us. Jesus and the Father release their Spirit of love into our hearts (Rm 5:5), so that we too may be able to love others as Jesus has. The Spirit brings us into an increased awareness of how truly beautiful we are in Jesus' love, which is the very image of the Father's love for us. Then He intercedes by calling us in His love to be with Christ a co-intercessor toward all human beings.

The Spirit makes us aware of our oneness with Christ, that in our wholeness and healthiness of divine life within us, we can go in haste to bring that same divinizing life to those members of the Body who are weak and dying from lack of full health. We are impelled to bring Jesus Christ, the Head, to the millions of human beings who do not know Him as Lord, God-Man.

Unfortunately, we can freely close ourselves off from the call of the Spirit to become intercessors with Christ. Thus, we can block off the relational intercession of the Holy Spirit which depends always on our cooperation. We need to distinguish a specific call of the Holy Spirit to embrace a style of life of heroic generosity, so filled with love of God and neighbor that such a person, day and night, lives as a *victim*, taking on the sins of the world in his oneness with the suffering Christ. This vocation is obviously not a universal call for all to embrace and can come only after long years of generous preparation and guidance by holy and well-balanced spiritual guides in harmony with the teachings of the Church.

Called To Love Is To Intercede

Yet, all Christians are called to love others as Jesus has. To love others has to imply a readiness to move beyond mere words or gestures and to embrace sacrifices as part of proving our love for others. "A man can have no greater love than to lay down his life for his friends" (Jn 15:13). Thus, as we offer up our prayers on behalf of others, living or deceased, we must be open to the Spirit leading us to make sacrifices to act out this loving concern.

We are free to choose to be Christian or not. But if we truly understand what it means to be a Christian and a living member building the Body of Christ by loving service, we have implicitly chosen to be intercessors, who offer prayers and sacrifices in loving oneness with Christ as He suffers in His members (Mk 9:29).

It is important to guard against our doing anything alone under our own power. We need to be constantly open to the Holy Spirit in order to be guided always by His power, prudence and love. He will inspire what sacrifices are to accompany our prayers of petitions in order that our love for others will be truly intercessory.

Filling Up The Sufferings Of Christ

Dietrich Bonhoeffer wrote, "When Christ calls a man, he bids him come and die" (*The Cost of Discipleship*, p. 99). This is nothing but to paraphrase the teaching of Christ reiterated in identical terms in the Synoptic Gospels:

> If anyone wants to be a follower of mine, let him renounce himself and take up his cross and follow me. For anyone who wants to save his life will lose it, but anyone who loses his life for my sake and for the sake of the gospel, will save it. (Mk 8:34. Cf. also: Mt 10:38, 16:24; Lk 9:23, 14:27)

But because of an unhealthy, negative contempt for the human body in medieval asceticism, suffering was self-imposed to bring about in the mind of the ascetic a sense of identity with the sufferings of Christ. All too often such sufferings were used by the intercessor as a point of "bargaining" with God for graces won for the sinful and lost.

Today, especially through biblical exegesis and deeper insights into the Pauline doctrine of the mystical body of Christ, we see the call to suffer with Christ as the inevitable result of obeying Christ against the kingdom of the "world."

St. Peter teaches us the necessity of suffering, not because we have done wrong, but out of obedience to Christ's teachings (1 P 3:14-17). If Jesus warned His disciples to expect persecutions for His Name's sake (Mt 10:16-25), then it is important to understand the relationship of sufferings and the communion within the body of Christ.

St. Paul boldly declares, "It makes me happy to suffer for you, as I am suffering now, and in my own body to do what I can to make up all that has still to be undergone by Christ for the sake of his body, the Church" (Col 1:24). This text has always been difficult to understand in its fullest sense. In what way can Paul or we think Christ's sufferings are incomplete and, therefore, we can fill them up? We must reject any false understanding that would assert Christ's personal sufferings in His passion and death were insufficient for our redemption and we would need to fill up the necessary sufferings.

Members Of The Body Of Christ

If we keep in mind St. Paul's powerful analogy of the Church as similar to a human body made up of many members and each member composed of cells that are interrelated with all other living cells of the entire body, then we can understand how Jesus extends His intercession through us to other members and to all human beings the world over, both among the living and the deceased.

Paul teaches, "If one part is hurt, all parts are hurt with it. If one part is given special honor, all parts enjoy it" (1 Co 12:26). Within the Body of Christ, therefore, we are all so interconnected since we have one Head, Jesus Christ, over us and His life, the Spirit, flows through all of us, bringing us a sharing in the very triune divine life. We share weaknesses, strengths, sufferings, as well as honors.

We have an example of this Pauline teaching in action, given by Pope St. Gregory the Great to the Bishop of Carthage at a time of great suffering in the African Church:

> By this charity, the same members, when personally afflicted, respond to the joy of others or, on the other hand, in personal joy they are consumed by the sorrows of others. The Master of the Gentiles, in fact, bears witness: "whether one member suffers, all the members suffer with it, or one member honored, all members rejoice with it. I do not doubt that you sigh for our distress while, you may be assured, we rejoice at your peace." (Letter 47)

We do not fill up the physical sufferings of Jesus' passion, but because we are tied one with Christ, we are able to suffer with Christ and fill up His sufferings as we work with Him in overcoming the evil of the Kingdom of darkness.

What Paul and the other early disciples, the martyrs, the living witnesses down to our present day, as Mother Teresa of Calcutta, Archbishop Oscar Romero, Cesar Chavez and even you and I suffer is still a continuation of what Christ first endured. We do not fill up anything lacking in His sufferings. In our apostolic ministry we are called to extend His sufferings by knowing ours are part of His, as we are a part of Him.

It is always in the context of our ministry that we become suffering intercessors, building up Christ's Body by joyfully accepting the sufferings that bring a new resurrectional life to individuals and to the entire Body of Christ, the Church. This is what Paul meant when he wrote these meaningful words:

> Indeed, as the sufferings of Christ overflow to us,
> so through Christ does our consolation overflow.
> When we are made to suffer, it is for your consola-

tion and salvation. When, instead, we are comforted, this should be a consolation to you, supporting you in patiently bearing the same sufferings as we bear. And our hope for you is confident, since we know that, sharing our sufferings, you will also share our consolation. (2 Co 1:5-7)

Building The Total Christ

The sufferings of us believers, therefore, are not independent of Christ's. As Christ once underwent His unique, individual sufferings, especially in His passion and death, so now He endures or shares in our daily sufferings, for He will always be one with the members of His Body, the Church. What we suffer out of love in His Spirit, He, as Head, also suffers in the same Spirit that makes Him one with His members.

Yet, we see that such sufferings have an eschatological effect. Such trials and tribulations bring about the future of the fulfilled Christ, the total Christ, the Head in His members. But, also, in the very moment of being accepted out of love for each other, we also share now in a corporate raising of the entire Body to a higher level of loving union.

Blood Of Martyrs—Seed Of Christianity

This is why instinctively from earliest times, Christians held in highest esteem the gift of martyrdom. To freely give one's life out of love for Christ and His message was considered as the highest, most perfect way of ministering to the Word preached to the world, as well as the most efficacious means of building by "edifying" the Church into the extension of the living, loving Jesus Christ, true God and true man.

St. Paul wished to bear his "chains" ultimately his impending martyrdom to build up the Church. "So I bear it all for the sake of those who are chosen, so that in the end they may have the salvation that is in Christ Jesus and the eternal glory that comes with it" (2 Tm 2:10). This witness to help others to be strengthened in their faith under trials, Paul powerfully highlights as he writes from his captivity to the Philippians. His text is worthy of our constant meditation:

My chains, in Christ, have become famous not only all over the Praetorium, but everywhere, and most of the brothers have taken courage in the Lord from these chains of mine and are getting more and more daring in announcing the Message without any fear. It is true that some of them are doing it just out of rivalry and competition, but the rest preach Christ with the right intention, out of nothing but love, as they know that this is my invariable way of defending the gospel. The others, who proclaim Christ for jealous or selfish motives, do not mind if they make my chains heavier to bear. But does it matter? Whether from dishonest motives or insincerity, Christ is proclaimed, and that makes me happy, and I shall continue being happy, because I know this will help to save me, thanks to your prayers and to the help which will be given to me by the Spirit of Jesus. My one hope and trust is that I shall never have to admit defeat, but that now as always I shall have the courage for Christ to be glorified in my body, whether by my life or by my death. Life to me, of course, is Christ, but then death would bring me something more, but then again, if living in this body means doing work which is having good results—I do not know what I should choose. I am caught in this dilemma: I want to be gone and be with Christ, which would be very much the better, but for me to stay alive in this body is a more urgent need for your sake. This weighs with me so much that I feel sure I shall survive and stay with you all, and help you to progress in the faith and even increase your joy in it, and so you will have another reason to give praise to Christ Jesus on my account when I am with you again. (Ph 1:13-26)

The power of intercessory prayer, through complete self-giving in sacrificial love even unto death, is brought out dramatically in the case of the first Christian martyr, St. Stephen. St. Luke in his account of the martyrdom of the first Christian martyr presents Stephen as teaching the "message" about Christ risen to glory, the conqueror of sin and death. For this he is to be stoned to death. Yet, "Stephen, filled with the Holy Spirit, gazed into heaven and saw the glory of God, and Jesus standing at God's right hand, 'I can see heaven thrown open and the Son of Man standing at the right hand of God.' The Jewish leaders rushed upon him and stoned him. But Stephen prayed, 'Lord Jesus, receive my spirit,' then he knelt down and said aloud, 'Lord do not hold this sin against them,' and with these words, he fell asleep. Saul entirely approved of the killing" (Ac 7:55-60).

Luke implies here that the Apostle to the Gentiles would receive the grace of conversion through the powerful intercessory prayer of Stephen, backed up by the heroic giving of his life in witness to the divinity of Jesus Christ.

Co-Priests With Christ The High Priest

The peak of our understanding of intercessory prayer and sacrifice is found in the teaching of Christ as the sole and perfect High Priest Who calls us to partake in a sharing of His one high priesthood. This is where we see true intercession on behalf of others as consisting ultimately in love offered to God in worshipful self-emptying sacrifice, united with the priestly-offering of Christ to the eternal Father on behalf of all of us.

We have already said that Jesus Christ alone is our Mediator. He came to die for our sins and, in the offering and sacrifice of Himself completely for us (Eph 5:2), He removes

114

our sinful condition before the heavenly Father and makes it possible that we can now have "communion" as children with the Father. Jesus still is our High Priest before the Father now and forever: "Jesus, made a high priest forever after the order of Melchisedek" (Heb 6:20).

Jesus Christ differs from all priests before Him in the Old Testament and after Him in the New Covenant. He is completely without sin. His sacrifice was made once and for all. He needs not to die for us again. But the amazing point of Jesus' priesthood is that the sacrifice He offers on our behalf is of Himself. He offers and is offered.

> Such a high priest, who is holy, harmless, undefiled, separate from sinners and higher than the heavens, does not need [like other high priests] to offer up sacrifice every day, first for his own sins and then for the people's, for he did this once when he offered up himself. (Heb 7:26-27)

Still, Jesus Christ calls everyone baptized in the name of the Trinity to share in His one priesthood. That priesthood consists in offering up in union with Jesus Christ spiritual sacrifices acceptable to God.

> You also, as lively stones, are built up a spiritual house, a holy priesthood, to offer up spiritual sacrifices, acceptable to God by Jesus Christ. . . . But you are a chosen generation, a royal priesthood, a holy nation, a peculiar people, that you should show forth the praises of him who has called you out of darkness into his marvelous light. (1 P 2:5, 9)

Besides the cultic priest of Christianity, ordained to renew the sacrifice of Christ and to gather up the united sacrifices of the Church that gather in Jesus Christ's name to mediate the mercy of the Father in the blood of His Son, each Christian is called upon by his/her Baptism to mediate the priesthood of Jesus Christ before the Father on their own behalf and that of their fellow beings.

We can participate in this priestly mediation to the degree that we have first allowed the priestly mediation of Jesus to have its full reconciling effects to come upon us and transform us according to the priestly heart of Christ.

Although we modern Christians know Jesus Christ alone is the Mediator of the human race with the Heavenly Father, yet we know through God's transforming grace what God has made of us. "And all things are of God who has reconciled us to himself by Jesus Christ and has given to us the ministry of reconciliation" (2 Co 5:18). We are called into the awesome redemptive work by the merits of Jesus Christ to reconcile the sinful world to God. Jesus Christ has worked a work of purification in us so we can already triumphantly cry out with St. Paul:

> I am crucified with Christ, nevertheless, I live, yet
> not I, but Christ lives in me and the life which I
> now live in the flesh, I live by the faith of the Son
> of God, who loved me and gave himself for me.
> (Ga 2:20)

Jesus Christ shares His divine life with us, as He lives in us as the vine is the life-giving source to the living branch. He is the Head. We, in whom Jesus lives, are the body. We are totally new in Him and share in His power to intercede before the throne of the Father. He "has raised us up together and made us sit together in heavenly places in Christ Jesus" (Eph 2:6). We have been empowered to use His merits and His Name, which is the only name whereby we shall be saved (Ac 4:12). It is His mediation, His intercession, that we share, as we, too, groan in the Spirit of Jesus on behalf of a race of a people that has forgotten God. Like Abraham, we beg, not on our own merits, but because of God's goodness made known through Jesus Christ, that men and women, cities and nations, the sick and suffering, the mentally confused and disturbed be spared and be healed and be reconciled with God.

116

Need Of Intercessors

Today, the world has desperate need for intercessors who mediate Jesus Christ and His intercessory power before the Father's throne on behalf of the human race. Jesus Christ wants to share His power, His love, His wisdom with the world, yet He still mediates His priestly mediation through human beings in whom He can have absolute power and freedom to work as He wishes. Absolute oneness with Christ does not make the Christian an intercessor distinct from Jesus Christ, but renders the mediation of Jesus Christ concretized in human terms on this earth.

As we are crucified with Christ Jesus, have died with Him, are justified with Him, made alive by Him, so we are raised with Him and are now seated with Him before the throne. All of our intercession comes from Jesus Christ. We are nothing; Jesus is all! There is only the High Priest, Jesus Christ. But still, we Christians, like St. John the Baptist, mediate Jesus Christ. We are constantly pointing out to others, "There is the Lamb of God. It is He Who takes away the sins of the world! He must increase. I must decrease. All glory be to the Lamb of God!"

> Unto him that loved us and washed us from our sins in his own blood and has made us kings and priests unto God and his Father. To him be glory and dominion forever and ever. Amen. (Rv 1:5-6)

Chapter Seven

THE EUCHARIST AND COMMUNION OF SAINTS

St. Augustine in his classic, *The City of God*, describes two different loves that have produced two different cities. "Two loves have made two cities: the love of self unto the hatred of God, and the love of God unto the hatred of one-self" (Ch. XIV; 28). Of these two loves, the one is holy while the other is impure. One is turned toward the neighbor, while the other is turned to oneself. The one thinks for the common good of the society that is above, the other bends the common good to one's own service in view of a prideful domination.

One is submitted to God, the other is jealous of Him. The one is tranquil, the other turbulent. The one is peaceful, the other is quarrelsome. The one prefers the truth to the praises of those who are self-seeking. The other is eager for praise of whatever sort. The one is a fashioner of friendship,

119

the other is envious. The one wishes well of his neighbor, that which he wishes for himself, while the other seeks to subdue his neighbor.

The one governs the others for their own good, the other for his own good. These two loves have in the beginning been manifested among the angels. The one among the good angels, the other among the wicked. And so among us human beings there have been these two distinct loves that have created two cities, that of the just and that of the wicked. These two cities have pursued their existence since the beginning of the angels, and of the human race, and will continue to do so until the end of time. They have intermingled, but on the day of final judgment there will be a complete separation.

I, The Vine, You, The Branches

Jesus has given us the allegory of the vine and the branches (Jn 15:1 ff.) to show the organic oneness of those who live united in His Spirit of love within His Body. Those who cut themselves off from His life flowing through them become like dead branches, fit only to be burned.

> As a branch cannot bear fruit all by itself,
> but must remain part of the vine,
> neither can you unless you remain in me.
> I am the vine,
> you are the branches.
> Whoever remains in me, with me in him,
> bears fruit in plenty,
> for cut off from me you can do nothing.
> Anyone who does not remain in me
> is like a branch that has been thrown away
> —he withers;
> these branches are collected and
>   thrown on the fire,
> and they are burnt.

If you remain in me
and my words remain in you,
you may ask what you will
and you shall get it.
It is to the glory of the Father
that you should bear much fruit,
and then you will be my disciples. (Jn 15:4-8)

In our first chapter, we started our search for a deeper understanding of the doctrine of the communion of saints by looking at our oneness in love with Jesus Christ. He is the Head and He forms one Body through His members, the living members who live in His loving Spirit. "Before anything was created, he existed, and he holds all things in unity. Now the Church is his body, he is its head" (Col 1:17-18).

The power of love is to unite what has been separated or divided. It brings into harmony and unity a diversity without destroying the differences. It, rather, exalts the diversity into a uniqueness so that the love of God is glorified in such individuated love for each of His creatures. The more you are raised by God's Spirit to the intimate presence of God, Father, Son and Spirit, living and loving within you with an infinite love, the more you and all the saints in Christ begin to enter into communion, a union with other human beings and, also, in union with all other creatures.

We have also pointed out that the early Fathers of the Church intermingled their understanding of the term *communion of saints* not only with an equal, but distinct, understanding of the term "saints," which included the sacraments, especially Baptism and the Eucharist, but also with the preaching of the Good News through the teaching authority in the Church. The consequent meaning of "communion of saints" referred, therefore, to members of the Body, those living and those in glory and those awaiting their fuller share in that same glory, as they lovingly served each other.

The formula, therefore, of the "communion of saints" never meant exclusively the sharing in the *sancta* or extensions of the humanity of Christ that sacramentally or symbolically aided in the building of the Body of Christ, nor exclusively the *sancti*, since each is contained in the other. But we have been focusing more primarily on this communion through the incarnation of Christ's divinity and humanity, as well as the extension through His Spirit of the means to divinize members of His Body into sharers of God's very own nature (2 P 1:4).

The Eucharist

In this chapter, we select one of the *sancta* or extensions of Jesus Christ, the Eucharist, as the goal and culmination of all other Christic communications in self-giving.

In all the sacraments, we can experience various *places* in our lives where we can encounter the dying-rising Jesus Christ. When we cooperate, and the visible rite is properly celebrated within the context of the Church through its teaching authority in union with the one, holy, catholic and apostolic community stemming from the Apostles, Jesus comes to us and brings us a new share in divine life. But, specifically, each sacrament brings us the divine life in a very special way so that we can more perfectly live our redeemed life in Christ within the context of the whole Body, the Church.

In the Eucharist, we receive Jesus as He prolongs His death and resurrection in us and within His Body, the Church. We receive His life that enables us to share in His death and resurrection in union with all the living and departed members of the same Body.

The Eucharist, therefore, is the peak of all other sacramental encounters with Christ. It brings us into perfect union with the dying-rising Christ of glory who makes us partakers in His life through the full release of His Spirit in His mysteries. He grants us fervor in the service of God, fidelity in the observance of His laws and ever-increasing sanctification manifested by our loving service toward all human beings.

The Eucharist completes all other sacraments insofar as it is already a sharing in the *parousia*, the final manifestation of the Lord in glory in perfect, surrendering service of Jesus Christ to the Father on our behalf. Although we are still pilgrims moving through the desert of life, nevertheless, the Eucharist guarantees and effects already a sharing in the final goal. The Eucharist is the full coming of the Lord in glory, the same as His final coming. And, yet, we must proclaim in the Eucharist His death and resurrection and His perfect glory until He comes. "Until the Lord comes, therefore, every time you eat this bread and drink this cup, you are proclaiming his death" (1 Co 11:26).

The Fullness Of God's Intimacy

Christ's eucharistic presence as Victim and Offerer, as perfect Priest and Martyr, as sublime Image of the heavenly Father's love for His children in Christ's *kenotic*, self-emptying love, is most perfectly symbolized in the Eucharist more than in any other "sancta" or holy "representation" of Him as Redeemer and Savior. Christ's eucharistic presence, however, must never be understood as just one form of His presence equal to His many other "presences" to us.

This can all too often happen, as we can easily observe in our Catholic tradition from the Middle Ages until the recent Vatican Council II. If we fail to understand the mystery of the Eucharist as the fullness, not only of God's self-emptying love for us, but as the fullness of the building up and completion of the entire plan of God's salvation, then we truly will not understand the Eucharist and the communion of saints. We can easily "objectivize" the Eucharist as a form of presence in a "place" where Jesus became present to individuals who receive Him in a space and a time where Jesus is present in "this" host or inside of that tabernacle "over there." And we will miss the full mystery of the Eucharist and the Body of Christ.

All other presences of Jesus in our material world (and

within the Church) meet in the Eucharist and are transcended and superseded by this unique presence. It is the climax of God's self-giving go us and, therefore, contains all other forms of God's presence "toward" us. In the Eucharist, God literally gives us a part of His very being as we receive the Body and Blood of Jesus Christ. St. Cyril of Alexandria in the fourth century wrote, "Fundamentally, the Eucharist is a victory — a victory of one who is absent to become present in a world which conceals him."

Now we have the means whereby we can enter into the fullness of God's intimate sharing of His very own life with us through touching the glorified, risen humanity of Christ in the Eucharist. Not only is it the entire, historical Jesus of Nazareth that we receive, but we receive the Risen Lord of glory with the presence of the Blessed Trinity.

Divine Energies Of Love

In the Eucharist, we find the most intense concentration of the Trinity's uncreated energies of love. As we partake of the glorified Body of Christ, we touch and are touched by the fullness of the Trinity. In the incarnation, God so loved the world as to give us His only begotten Son (Jn 3:16). Out of this mystery of His infinite love flows the Eucharist as the "place" where we, individually, and also as the community, the Body of Christ, can encounter the Trinity in their individual, personal relations as Father, Son and Holy Spirit.

Who sees the Son sees also the Father (Jn 14:9). Who receives the body and blood of the Son of God receives not only the Son, but also the Father in His Spirit of love. Who abides in the Son abides in the Father Who comes with the Son and His Spirit to dwell within the recipient of the Eucharist (Jn 14:23). Thus, the mystery of the Eucharist brings us into the fullness of God's energizing love for us in the resurrection, the death and the incarnation that returns us to the Source of all reality, the beginning of the very process of

God's self-giving to human and angelic beings in the Trinity, even before creation.

In our oneness with Jesus Christ in the Eucharist, therefore, we are brought into the heart of the Trinity. Here is the climax of God's eternal plan when He "chose us in Christ, to be holy and spotless, and to live through love in his presence" (Ep 1:4). Sin destroys that image and likeness to Jesus Christ within us. Our own sinfulness, added to the effects of original sin, hinders the Holy Spirit from raising us to an awareness in grace that Jesus truly lives in us and we in Him. But the Eucharist (here we see the need of careful preparation to receive worthily this sacrament by repentance and an authentic *metanoia* or conversion) restores and powerfully builds up this oneness with Christ.

Incorporated Into Christ

St. Paul especially emphasizes in his writings our *incorporation* into Christ. And the early Fathers understood that St. Paul meant this to be a literal union, a true incorporation into Christ's very own substantial, divine life. By the cross, Christ destroyed eschatological death and sin. By His own resurrectional life, which we receive in the Eucharist, He brings to us this "new life," effecting a new oneness with Him through His Holy Spirit.

> When he died, once for all, to sin, so his life now
> is life with God, and in that way, you too must consider yourselves to be dead to sin but alive for God
> in Christ Jesus (Rm 6:10-11).

Baptism, according to St. Paul, puts us into direct contact with the risen, glorified Christ Who, now, through His spiritualized Body-Person, can come and truly dwell within us, especially through the Eucharist. We form with Christ, one Body, He the Head, we, His members.

The blessing cup that we bless is a communion with

the blood of Christ and the bread that we break is a communion with the body of Christ. The fact that there is only one loaf means that, though there are many of us, we form a single body because we all have a share in this one loaf. (1 Co 10:16-17)

The first and greatest effect of the Eucharist is to bring us into a oneness with the trinitarian community of love. Through the intensification of our union with the risen Jesus, the Holy Spirit brings us into a new awareness of our being, also, one with the Father and the Holy Spirit. This is the essence of the Last Supper Farewell Discourse of Jesus, as recorded in St. John's Gospel (Jn 17:20-23). The glory that the Father gave to Jesus through His death-resurrection is to raise His humanity into a oneness with His "natural" state of being the only begotten Son of the Father from all eternity.

United With The Father And Spirit

In the Eucharist, Jesus shares this glory with us so that, through the power of the Holy Spirit, we are able to experience not only our oneness with Jesus, but our oneness as sharers in His Sonship. St. Cyril of Alexandria summarizes the common teaching of the early Fathers, showing that our divinization in the Eucharist brings about a union with the very Trinity:

> Accordingly, we are all one in the Father and in the Son and in the Holy Spirit, one I say, in unity of relationship of love and concord with God and one another . . . one by conformity in godliness, by communion in the sacred body of Christ, and by fellowship in the one and Holy Spirit and this is a real, physical union. (*Commentary on St. John's Gospel*)

If Jesus and the Father abide in each other and have come to abide within us in the Eucharist (Jn 14:23), the Holy Spirit,

126

as the bond of unity that brings them together and who proceeds from their abiding union as love, also comes and dwells in us. St. Paul refers to this reality when he writes, "Your body, you know, is the temple of the Holy Spirit, who is in you since you received him from God" (1 Co 6:19).

One Body

Not only does the Eucharist bring us into a realized oneness with the Father, Son and Holy Spirit, but this oneness in many effects a powerful, new experience of our oneness with angelic and human beings. To understand this, we must see how St. Paul uses this term *body*. He usually uses the Greek word for body, *soma*, to refer to the historical body of Jesus, which the Apostles saw and touched. That body rose from the dead, the whole Body-Person, Jesus Christ, living in His new resurrectional life.

His body is also given as food in the Eucharist. This is a different modality of existence, but it flows out from and contains the resurrectional Body-Person, Jesus Christ. Jesus' body in St. Paul's writings also refers to His Church, of which He is the Head and His Christian members, who live in His divine life through the Spirit, are true parts of this Body.

We can say that there is absolute identity between the historical and the risen Jesus Christ. The Body of Christ referring to the total Church with Christ as the Head cannot be ontologically identical, since the very life infusing the members, making them living parts of Christ's Body, is identical with the divine life of the physical Christ. Even though we Christians, in Baptism and the Eucharist and through other means of receiving grace, partake of the same divine life, we still remain ourselves with our own human personalities and life.

The Church that reaches the peak of its oneness with the glorified Christ in the Eucharist is one in the union between Christ the Head and the individual members. Christ's bodily, risen, human nature is the point of contact between Christ and the church members. Christ is the Head of the Body-Church not only by His authority that He imparts to His church teachers and pastors, but by being the principle of life, the one who gives nourishment and sustenance so that the members can live in Him. ". . . Christ who is the head by whom the whole body is fitted and joined together, every joint adding its own strength" (Ep 4:16).

In strong, dramatic language St. Augustine captures this oneness with Christ to indicate that this union between Christ and His members is more than merely a moral union:

> Let us rejoice and give thanks that we have become, not only Christians, but Christ. My brothers, do you understand the grace of God our Head? Stand in admiration, rejoice; we have become Christ.

The Eucharist most perfectly expresses the union between Christ and its members in the one Mystical Body of Christ. And it is principally in this sacrament that this union is effected. He loves us in the oneness of the infinite, uncreated energies of love of the Trinity. We join our hearts to that of the God-Man and praise and worship the heavenly Father with a perfect love and in complete self-surrender. At no time in the Christian's life is he or she united more powerfully with the power and the glory of Christ risen than in the eucharistic union.

Oneness With Each Other

In the Eucharist, we are not only united with the Trinity, but we attain a new oneness with the others in whom the same trinitarian life lives, especially within the context of the eucharistic celebration. It is here that the Church, the Body of Christ, comes together in loving union with its Head, Jesus Christ. The Liturgy, or the "work" of the People of God, is the sacred place and time when the Church is most impregnated by the power of the Holy Spirit. It is the realization of the reason for which it exists: to praise and glorify God for the gifts of life and salvation which we have received and to become a gift of God's gifts of life to others whom we lovingly serve.

It is especially in the reception of the Eucharist that all members of Christ's Body are most powerfully united in a new sense of oneness with one another. They symbolically, but really, enter into the depths of the richness of God's self-sacrificing love. The Eucharist is not only a sacrament, it is also the ever-now sacrifice of Christ for us to the Father unto our healing and redemption. It is the culmination of all the sacraments, for in the Eucharist Jesus Christ gives Himself as He did in the first eucharistic celebration of the Last Supper before His death and as He did on the cross.

To Be Eucharist

The divinizing power of the Trinity experienced in the Eucharist is to be the power that drives us outward toward other communities to be Eucharist, bread broken, to give ourselves not only as Jesus did in our behalf, but with Jesus and the Father abiding within us with their Spirit of love. The Trinity empowers us to do what would be impossible for us alone to do consistently.

The Eucharist is the Bread of Life to be shared with others. Have we really lifted our hearts to God, if we have not offered Him our whole being, with our whole set of relationships to other people who touch us and whom we touch in daily life? Of what avail is our suffering in the community's Liturgy, if it is not completed in the suffering in our daily living on behalf of others?

Our participation and sharing in the Body of Christ in the Eucharist are measured by the degree of sharing ourselves with one another before the Father of us all. St. Paul's vision of the Body of Christ, as manifest especially through the Eucharist, shows us to be many members with Christ as our Head. We all have received a variety of gifts but always the same Holy Spirit Who builds us all in the gift of love into the same, one Body of Christ, the Church (1 Co 12:4; Ep 4:4). Such gifts are to be exercised in love through self-giving, through sacrificial love, even unto death. This means that, as Christ went out to minister in love to the needs, bodily, psychical and spiritual, of those whom He met, so we are to go forth from the Eucharist with the power of the risen Jesus within us to minister with Him to the needs of all whom we meet. His Spirit breaks down any separation between members of the Body of Christ whether they are in glory, in expectant purification of purgatory, or are still with us on this earth.

The Eucharist And The Church

Permit me to lead you into a deeper theological understanding of the relationships between the Eucharist and the Church in order that we might arrive at a greater understanding of how the Eucharist brings about the most intimate communion of the saints. First, we need to understand that Jesus Christ is the sole Offerer and Victim. The Church, the Bride of Christ, is born on Calvary through the opened heart of Christ, as analogically, Eve, the "mother of the living," was brought forth from the side of Adam.

Therefore, Jesus alone offers Himself as sacrifice on Calvary and as sacrament of love. The first Apostles at the Last Supper did not co-offer their sacrifice with that of Christ. The Church, constituted by the college of the Apostles in the upper room, and the Church, born through the death-resurrection of Jesus on Calvary, is the receiver of the sacrifice and sacrament of Christ.

Yet, Jesus told His disciples, "This is my body which will be given for you; do this as a memorial of me" (Lk 22:19). We Christians meet to celebrate this salutary precept of a memorial of the one and only sacrifice that takes away our sins. In this memorial the Church makes the one and only sacrifice of Christ "present" in all places and for all times on this earth as in heaven. The Church, the extension of Christ, his very own Body connected with the glorified Jesus Christ, also offers herself as Body with Christ as Head, as Offerer and Victim. Therefore, in each valid Mass or Liturgy, the victim and the offerer are two-fold: both Christ and the Church.

Thus, we see how the Mass can never be conceived of only vertically as an act of a duly-ordained priest or minister without, also, the ecclesial aspect of the horizontal, extension of Christ, the Church, also one with the Victim and Offerer, Jesus Christ. If the members of the Church are not also offering themselves along with their Head, Jesus, the Liturgy is a caricature of what Christ intended when He created and poured out His Spirit upon her. Now Christ does not ascend alone from this earth. He must be accompanied always by His Church, His Bride. The Head cannot stand alone without His Body.

The Church stands united with the Headship of Christ and appeals before the heavenly Father to the infinite grace of Christ's historical sacrifice. But she also ascends to the throne of God as victim, immolated, and offered, like Christ, but also with Christ.

St. Augustine in an outstanding manner captured this ecclesial aspect of the Church offering herself along with Christ to the Father. He writes:

> But for me, it is good to cling to God: now it is a fact that the entire redeemed city, that is, the congregation and the society of saints, is offered to God like a universal offering through the high priest, who offered himself in the passion for us . . . . This is the sacrifice of Christians: many are one body of Christ. And this is celebrated by the Church in the sacrament of the altar, well-known to the faithful, where it is made plain to her that in that, which she offers, she herself is offered. (*The City of God*, Ch. X, 20)

We can see why from the earliest centuries the offertory

of the gifts of the faithful encouraged the participants to enact in their daily lives the oneness of being a sacrifice, a victim, and a sacrament of love, in loving service to those in need. We can see how the communion of the angels and saints in the Body of Christ triumphant also participate in offering themselves and living out that "oblation" in loving service to the other members of the Body, especially in their sacrificial, intercessory prayer for those in need on earth and those departed in their purgatorial therapy.

How beautifully in the gift of the Eucharist the ascending movement of the Church (God's new creation in Christ) and the descending movement of the heavenly Father both meet in the one person of the Eucharist, Jesus Christ. We must ponder this tremendous truth, that the Church makes the Eucharist through "commemorating" actively the memorial of Christ's sacrifice on the cross and, yet, the Eucharist makes the Church. The Body is one with the Head in sharing in the priesthood of Christ as victim and offerer. Yet, the Body becomes more the Body, more Christ, precisely in and through the Eucharist.

We keep ever in mind that, though we, the Church, do this in "memory" of Him, the Church's Eucharist, her sacrifice, as sacrifice, comes only from Christ. The primary origin of this sacrifice and of salvation is always the action of Christ. As members of the Church, the priestly people and the ordained priest offer the sacrifice of Christ and themselves only because of the power of Christ given through His Spirit to His members.

The Church Offers

We have touched earlier in this chapter on the various meanings we can attach in the Eucharist to the concept, *Body of Christ*. The concrete Body of Christ or offering Church of the Eucharist can likewise be understood on three levels. Which is the real offerer in union with Christ of the Eucharist: the concrete congregation gathered around a bishop or priest, the local church, the diocese, or the universal, world-wide Church that would, somehow, also embrace the angels and saints?

Pope Paul VI, in his encyclical, *Mysterium Fidei*, on the Eucharist (1965), gives us this opinion: "It helps to realize that it is nothing less than the whole Church which, in union with Christ in His role as priest and victim, offers the sacrifice of the Mass and is offered in it. The Fathers of the Church taught this wondrous doctrine . . . " (*Mysterium Fidei,* ·p. 13, St. Paul Publications). Karl Rahner responds to this statement of Pope Paul VI: "It cannot be proved that acts of that kind (corporate acts) are posited in relation to a particular Mass by any human being other than those who in some way are really engaged in the particular sacrifice itself. . . . To suppose they are posited is nothing but pious fantasy" (*The Celebration of the Eucharist,* p. 42).

I must agree with Rahner that it is a contradiction in terms of fulfilling Christ's precept to do this eucharistic act as a memorial in His memory and to state that the entire Church with all her members co-offer every single Mass. Those not actually present are not fulfilling the injunction of Christ to be actively a part of commemorating the sacrifice of Christ by adding their one individual and corporate contribution as victim and offerer.

We should, however, say that every Mass or Liturgy is offered in the name of the entire Church. An officiating priest and the congregation with him are never acting as individuals but, rather, as ecclesial members of the entire Body, the Church. The universal Church can be said to be present in the individual congregation and local church as in a sign. A given congregation, celebrating the Eucharist, can be said to be the incarnation and extension in concrete actualization of the entire universal Church.

Fellowship Of The Holy Spirit

If the Eucharist's fruit is the *koinonia* or fellowship of the Holy Spirit through the death-resurrection of Jesus Christ, then the Spirit's work is to actualize the unity of the faithful. This is the teaching of St. Paul:

> Bear with one another charitably, in complete self-lessness, gentleness and patience. Do all you can to preserve the unity of the Spirit by the peace that binds you together. There is one Body, one Spirit, just as you were all called into one and the same hope when you were called. There is one Lord, one faith, one baptism, and one God who is Father of all, over all, through all and within all. (Ep 4:2-6)

Not only is there a surge of unifying love from the Holy Spirit released among the participants of a given Liturgy, but there is a release of the fruit of the Spirit (Ga 5:22).

We cannot truly celebrate the death and resurrection of Christ in the Liturgy unless we move away from our own individualistic absorption to enter the very mind of Christ. "Do this as a remembrance of me" (Lk 22:19) is a command of Christ to recall what He did, what He always is doing in liturgical time, and to do this in His presence and power. The celebration of Mass is, therefore, the action of Christ and His people, each taking his/her appointed place and role in His Body, being of one heart and mind with Christ as victim and offerer.

In celebrating the Liturgy from the introductory rites of antiphons, penitential and other prayers to the Liturgy of the Word, to the Eucharist of offertory, consecration and communion, all is ordered that the Eucharist may be a living sign of our sharing in Christ's sacrifice and sacrament of love. The Eucharist is not only a sign of our union with Jesus Christ and the Heavenly Father by the illumination of the Spirit of love but, above all, of our union or our desire to work lovingly toward union with all human beings.

Apostolic Service

In communion with Jesus but, also, with the Father and the Holy Spirit, the Christian community, individually and

134

corporately, is grafted on to the paschal mystery. Its weaknesses and sinfulness are entrusted to the strength of Jesus the Healer. The elements of death and division in it are transmuted into factors of life and unity. Love, the gift of the Spirit (Rm 5:5), transforms hearts and effects communion among them at the deep level of faith, hope and love.

Energized by the oneness thus produced, love then issues forth into dynamic, apostolic service keyed to respond to contemporary needs on the horizontal level. Thus, our dedication to these needs springs out of the heart of our community with one another in the one Body of Christ. What makes the church community unique over all other human communities is the common faith, hope and love received in Baptism and activated intensely in the Eucharist through the release of the Spirit of the Risen Lord that allow each member to become incorporated into this community, that is truly the very Body of the Risen Lord Jesus. We are enjoined to become what we have eaten, to become the fullness of the very Body of Christ the Church through service of self-emptying love toward others in the power of the Eucharistic Christ Whom we have received.

The Liturgy, carried out to perfection exteriorly, will be but a tinkling cymbal in the ears of God, unless we who celebrate it continue to glory in the same Lord also in the economic, social, political and cultural fields. Our intense participation in community prayer and sharing in the Body of Christ in the Eucharist is measured by the degree of our sharing ourselves with each other before the Father of us all.

For one who has recognized in the Liturgy, Christ, in bread and wine, such an act of faith continues as he sees on each human being the mark of the sacred blood of Jesus Christ. For the Christian contemplative going forth from the Eucharist, there is no insignificant event that does not bear the stamp of the Holy Trinity's desire to redeem all creation and restore it through Christ to the original plan as conceived by that loving community of the Trinity. We share in Christ's high priestly power as we, in love, do all to transform the raw stuff of this world into His Body. This is not only to celebrate the Eucharist but, above all, to live it.

Unity With The Angels And The Saints

Thus, the Liturgy extends through the memorial of Christians on earth the gift of the participants in the supreme gift of Christ to the historical world. But the same Liturgy opens up Christians celebrating the death-resurrection of Christ to a living unity with the angelic powers and human saints in glory. This we can call the *eschatological* aspect of the Body of Christ, which the Eucharist makes most real for us on earth in the most intense fellowship with those already in glory.

The Liturgy also brings us into a oneness in service with our departed loved ones still in need of healing in order to enter into the fullness of glory of Christ's death and resurrection. We cannot separate, as we have pointed out, the Church Triumphant from the Church Suffering from the Church Militant. The Eucharist's fruit is to bring us into a unity in Christ's Body that embraces equally all those living in Christ.

Let us now, first, look at our communion with the angels and saints, which reaches its peak of oneness in the Eucharist. The eschatological aspect of the Eucharist highlights the "already" of the Kingdom of God. It calls out joy and thanksgiving from the hearts of those celebrating the Eucharist for the gifts of the angelic spirits who have already arrived at the state of loving service that shares in the martyrdom and passover of Jesus, the High Priest.

In celebrating the Divine Liturgy the angels allow us to be lifted up in the Spirit to the eternal *kairos* of God's salvific time where we already share in the highest communion possible, continued praise, worship and surrendering oblation to serve the Lord of Hosts.

This is beautifully expressed in the ancient 4th century Liturgy of St. John Chrysostom in the Preface:

136

. . . We thank you also for this sacrifice which you are pleased to receive from our hands, even though there stand before you thousands of archangels and myriads of angels, Cherubim and Seraphim, six-winged and many-eyed, borne aloft on their wings, who . . . sing, proclaim, cry out and chant the triumphal hymn.

And all members of the celebrating community with the angels and saints together chant the hymn recorded in the vision of the prophet Isaiah:

Holy, holy, holy, Lord of Hosts! Heaven and earth are filled with your glory. Hosanna in the highest! Blessed is he who comes in the name of the Lord. Hosanna in the highest!

Union with the heavenly spirits is highlighted also in the Great Entrance of the same Liturgy. The concelebrating priests and deacons recite, while the people sing the "Cherubim Hymn":

Let us who here mystically represent the Cherubim in singing the thrice-holy hymn to the life-giving Trinity, . . . let us now lay aside every earthly care . . . so that we may welcome the King of the universe who comes escorted by the invisible armies of angels. Alleluia, alleluia, alleluia!

United With The Saints Who Have Been Made Perfect

All Christian Liturgies continue the faith vision that allows the Christian community to enter into the presence not only of the angelic spirits, but also of the human saints who have already entered into glory to the degree that they have suffered with Christ. These Liturgies and the faith exercised by the participants in the eucharistic Liturgy find a basis for such union between those Christians still on earth and those human beings called saints in the Letter to the Hebrews.

"With so many witnesses in a great cloud on every side of us, we, too, then, should throw off everything that hinders us, especially the sin that clings so easily, and keep running steadily in the race we have started" (Hebr 12:1-2). The Holy Spirit in the Eucharist not only binds us living on this earth together with each other, but also binds us with the victorious human spirits who have already reached that heavenly city of Mount Sion.

Celebrating the eucharistic banquet always brings the participants, as we have already pointed out, into the eschatological aspect of the goal and fulfillment of God's salvific plan. The same Letter to the Hebrews brings us into the Spirit that permeates the union between those in Christ still living on this earth and those who have died in the odor of sanctity:

> But what you have come to is Mount Zion and the city of the living God, the heavenly Jerusalem where the millions of angels have gathered for the festival, with the whole Church in which everyone is a "first-born son" and a citizen of heaven. You have come to God himself, the supreme Judge, and been placed with the *spirits of the saints* who have been made perfect, and to Jesus, the mediator who brings a new covenant and a blood for purification which pleads more insistently than Abel's. (Hebr 12:22-24)

Hope For Us Who Still Are Pilgrims

What we find in the prayers offered in the Christian Liturgies on behalf of the Saints are the often-repeated remembrance of their faith and good works, a plea to God through Christ and the merits of the saints that we on earth might imitate them in their holiness and praise to God for them. There is explicit faith that, as the Book of Revelation states, the saints have attained the goal of integration, of "resting" from their labors, since their good deeds go with them and become the basis of their continued loving service to intercede on our behalf. "Happy are those who die in the Lord! Happy, indeed, the Spirit says; now they can rest forever after their work, since their good deeds go with them" (Rv 14:12).

Their good deeds have made them what they are as persons in the Body of Christ. They still live in active service according to their oneness with Christ. They still extend the Kingdom of God through their intercessory, oblational sharing in the sacrifice of Christ and the offering of themselves to bring to us the presence of their Head, and ours, Jesus Christ. This double aspect of rejoicing in their triumph with Christ in glory and their continued power to intercede on our behalf is highlighted in the prayer (Collect) of the Mass of All Saints, November 1, in the Roman Catholic Liturgy:

> Father, all-powerful and ever-living God,
> today we rejoice in the holy men and women
> of every time and place.
> May their prayers bring us your forgiveness and
>   love.
> We ask this through our Lord Jesus Christ.

Imitation Is Communion

In the oneness that we manifest between ourselves on earth and the saints already in glory, we reach a communion that brings us into a present reality that fills us with joy in their successes and attained goal and which challenges us to imitate them. Such prayers in the Liturgy that praise and honor the saints for their holy lives of words and actions bring about a communion when we are edified by their witness of a Christ-like life and, through their intercession, we are called out to imitate their examples in our own lives.

It was St. Ambrose who wrote, "When we imitate, we

139

commune" (*Commentary on the Epistle to the Romans*). It is in our desire to live as the saints did that measures the degree of our loving union with them. They become for us a gift from God, an extension of Jesus Christ in glory, a hope of what can be our future.

To pray to and honor St. Paul is to want also to be one with him by imitating his zeal to win the entire world to Christ. To honor St. Stephen is not only to pray for his intercession, but already to have the strength to forgive all our enemies. Just as we cannot pray to Christ, the great Intercessor, without also wanting to have a share in His sufferings by imitating Him, so we also cannot be satisfied in the Liturgy to pray for gifts through the intercession of the saints without also wanting to imitate them in their share in the sufferings and death of Jesus Christ. Honor and celebration go together with communion and imitation of the saints who still hold out the sign of victory that is their present oneness in Christ's glory. We must always see our oneness and our devotion to the saints in the light of our oneness with Jesus Christ, the Head of the Body, of which the saints, along with us, are members.

Growth By Loving Service

Once we can transcend the static vision of heaven as an "old folks' home of retirement" and see the true communion that exists between the healthy members of the Body of Christ and their desire to continue to do all to bring the weak and the sick into the fullness of life, the more we will see that the saints rejoice in seeking lovingly to serve us in our needs. They exercise God's immense love burning within them by letting it out in loving service to the needy ones, both to those of us in this earthly existence and to those who are in need of the healing therapy of purgatory.

The saints eagerly share their highly developed charisms with others, all in order to bring Christ to full maturity in His Body. If the union effected in the Eucharist binds us to the

140

saints and obtains for us their powerful witness and intercession, we should also want to pray for and be of service to them. But how can we pray *for* the saints who already are triumphant in glory? As the saints answer our prayers through their intercessory sharing in Christ's mediation, so we can pray *for* them in a similar manner: that they and we and all God's children might attain unto the fullness of happiness, glory and maturity in Christ.

Praying **For** *The Saints*

In many of the ancient Eastern Liturgies, as typified by that of the Byzantine Liturgy of St. John Chrysostom of the 4th century, we find a rather strange (at least to our minds) expression of our relationship to the saints in glory. After the consecration of the Gifts, the priest offers this prayer on behalf of the Church and the people present at the Eucharist:

> Moreover, we offer you this spiritual and bloodless sacrifice for our forefathers in the faith who have gone to their rest, for the fathers, patriarchs, prophets, apostles, preachers, evangelists, martyrs, confessors, ascetics and for every just soul that has died in the faith . . . . And, especially, for our most holy, most pure, most blessed and glorious Lady, the Mother of God . . . . and ever-virgin Mary.

There follow prayers for which this sacrifice is also offered: "*for* St. John the Baptist, *for* the most-renowned Apostles, and *for* all your saints through whose prayers may you visit us, O God."

We do not offer the Eucharistic sacrifice *for* the saints in the sense of "*to* them," as the recipients of our adoration. St. Augustine is very strong in rejecting this interpretation. "It is not to them, God forbid! But to God that we offer sacrifices . . . " (Sermon 273, 7). Nicholas Cabasilas, a fourteenth-century Byzantine theologian, clarifies this preposition, "*for* the saints," by explaining that it is a general act of thanksgiving and praise to God for the great gifts they are to the Church. He writes of this blessing that the saints are for us:

> The proof is still that the definitive sanctity of the saints is God's greatest gift to men. And this is why it is inconceivable that the Church should not give thanks to him for it. What am I saying? The definitive sanctity of the saints is the greatest of God's gifts? It represents all that God has to give us. For of all the good things that he has done unto our race, this is the end and the fruit: the society of the saints. (*Explanation of the Divine Liturgy*)

Not only do we honor and thank them for their example of how to live a true Christian life by suffering even now in order to enter into glory with Christ (Rm 8:17), but we rejoice as we too wish to share in their sufferings by living out our share in the sacrifice of Christ and His sacrament of love.

Inflamed With Yearning

St. Bernard, in a sermon on the Feast of All Saints, explains this eschatological aspect of our communion with the saints in the Liturgy, after pointing out that the saints in glory do not seek our earthly honors when they possess already the honors of the heavenly Father Himself. He then points out how we need to call to mind the saints for our own benefit:

> Clearly, if we venerate their memory, it serves us, not them. But I tell you, when I think of them, I feel myself inflamed by a tremendous yearning.
>
> When we commemorate the saints we are inflamed with another yearning: that Christ our life may also appear to us as he appeared to them and that we may one day share in his glory.
>
> Therefore, we should aim at attaining this glory

with a wholehearted and prudent desire. That we may rightly hope and strive for such blessedness, we must above all seek the prayers of the saints. Thus, what is beyond our own powers to obtain will be granted through their intercession. (Sermon 2: *On All Saints' Day*)

We, therefore, pray *"for* the saints" by way of thanksgiving that God has brought to such completion their Baptism through their sharing during their earthly life in death to selfishness in order to put on a oneness with Jesus Christ, that reflected itself in their daily lives of loving service for others and, even now, in their glorified lives, as they live with burning zeal to lay down their lives in love for us in our great need.

Where more intensely can the Body of Christ meet, than in the sacrament of love and commemoration of the sacrifice of Christ? It is only natural that we should yearn in our commemoration of the saints, to receive their powerful intercession. We offer our sacrifices in that union of the entire Body of Christ and are encouraged by the help and the oneness with the great ones, to help us also attain greater oneness with Christ and oneness with the total Christ in His fulfilled Body, the Church.

Helping The Departed Souls In Purgatory

In all Christian Liturgies, especially those of the early Church, the Eucharist is the most intense experience of the praying community on earth with Christ in His other members, the saints and the departed, who are still undergoing healing therapy of any remnants of self-centeredness. Therefore, there have always existed within these Liturgies places for commemorating the departed loved ones to hasten the moment when they, too, will enter into the fullness of Christ's glory. Remembering the saints, we have said, stresses the eschatological goal toward which all members of Christ's Body, the Church, are called.

By offering prayers in commemoration of our departed loved ones, we join in loving sacrifice with Christ, our Head, and the saints and angels, to express our lively hope in the expectation of full oneness of these loved ones in purgatory. The Eucharistic Prayer I (*The Roman Canon*) offers this prayer for the departed: "Remember, Lord, those who have died and have gone before us marked with the sign of faith, especially those for whom we now pray [specific persons departed are commemorated by the priest and faithful]. May these, and all who sleep in Christ, find in your presence light, happiness and peace."

We have pointed out that the Divine Liturgy is the enactment in human time of the eternal *now* sacrifice of Jesus Christ offered to the heavenly Father on behalf of the living and the dead. Jesus Christ is alway interceding with illimitable power for all the members of His Body at whatever stage of development they are. The Church, in her sacrifice of Christ, extends the sacrifice of Christ Who takes away sins. The Church prays that God may pardon and purify the deceased persons of all their sins. To understand the value of offering Liturgies for the deceased and of assisting fervently at the celebration, we must understand that the Church is in the most intimate union with Christ. He is the Head, we are His members.

We are privileged in the celebration of the Divine Liturgy to offer, not only the Church's official prayers for the departed loved ones, but to offer our own particular prayers. Such prayers are not to be merely magical expressions that allow us to hope that our loved ones can be released from the fires of purgatory quickly through our petitions. The Liturgy and the prayers that you offer for a beloved deceased are beginning points of a love process whereby you with Christ live the sacrifice of the cross in your daily life on behalf of your departed loved ones. To live the Eucharist in their regard is the best way of helping your beloved departed. The Divine Liturgy directs the love of Christ toward those still suffering in hopeful expectation of becoming purified of all

144

isolation and self-centeredness to enjoy a greater share of the resurrectional glory with Christ.

One Breath, One Body

Thus, we see how the Eucharist not only sacramentally symbolizes, but also effects what it symbolizes. In the memorial of Christ's passion, death and resurrection, we enter into His perfect sacrifice, effected once on Calvary, but now extended as we become one Body, sharing the very body and blood of Christ.

The effects of the Eucharist, wrought by the Holy Spirit and our own cooperation, as we seek to live more in Christ "in truth and love," are not only to unite us more with Christ but with other living and departed members of Christ's Body, as well. Pope St. Leo highlights the awesome responsibility of living the Eucharist we have received by becoming Christ to all God's creatures. "The sharing in the body and Blood of Christ has no other effect than to turn and change us into what we receive" (*Sermon 63, 7*). St Paul also expresses this union between Christ and all of us members effected in the Eucharist: "The blessing-cup that we bless is a communion with the blood of Christ, and the bread that we break is a communion with the body of Christ. The fact that there is only one loaf means that, though there are many of us, we form a single body because we all have a share in this one loaf" (1 Co 10:16-18).

We are born spiritually as God's children, brothers and sisters to each other, as we truly live the sacrament of Baptism that reaches its fullness of loving union between us and God and between all human brothers and sisters in the Eucharist. In the Old Covenant, the blood of goats and bulls and the ashes of heifers were sprinkled on those who incurred defilement and they were restored to the holiness of their outward lives.

How much more effectively the blood of Christ, who offered himself as the perfect sacrifice to God through the eternal Spirit, can purify our inner self from dead actions so that we do our service to the living God. (Hebr 9:13-14)

Chapter Eight

HEAVEN: A LOVING PROCESS OF CONTINUED GROWTH

We come now to view the meaning of the doctrine of the communion of saints in regard to heaven, the final goal of God's creation. We have seen in the last chapter that the communion of saints contains two elements. The first consists in the intercessory prayer and sacrificial love, one with the crucified Christ, of all members of the body of Christ, as they lovingly seek to extend the healing love of Jesus to those in need.

The second is the *eschatological*, final goal of all God's creatures, of greatest unity in diversity in the communion of saints, which we call *heaven*. Whatever *com-union* (union with) there is among the members of Christ in the Church still in pilgrimage through historical time and space, we all stretch out into the far future when there will be no more time and space, as we have known and experienced them in our material existence.

There has always been in the hearts of human beings a

desire to ponder what the future of our lives and of the entire world will be. Today, more than ever, with advanced technology available, we moderns are becoming even more concerned about the future. "Futurology" is the science that seeks to understand the future and to provide tools whereby we can obtain greater control over our destiny. The surface of planet earth is exploding with developing sciences and technologies, but the efforts to harness these skills, to develop the earth's resources, and to share them with other inhabitants in peace and love, have met largely with uncoordinated helter-skelter results.

The difference between sheer science about the future and what the Church, through divine revelation has taught in its knowledge about the future of the world, is the difference between simple growth toward fruition and the need of something *new* to enter into the process. Jesus Christ risen is that something new, that life-giving leaven, that has entered into the potentiality of the universe. This is what is called in theology *eschatology*. This is the part of theology that raises questions concerning the end of our lives and of the entire world. It is derived from the Greek word *eschaton*, which means the *end*, or the last things. It usually concerns such questions as death, judgment, heaven, hell, purgatory, resurrection of the dead, and the *parousia*, or the second coming of Christ.

Parousia: Christ's Second Coming

Christ is risen and is in glory before the throne of His heavenly Father. The saints and angels also share in His eternal glory. Yet, other members within the body of Christ still live in the "not yet." The Church has always, from the original followers' experience of Jesus' first "unveiling" in the appearances recorded in the New Testament, longingly looked forward to a full "unveiling." *Parousia* is the Greek word that the Church uses to describe that second coming of Christ in glory at the end of time.

We live in tensioned-waiting for the full manifestation of the total Christ, Jesus, the Head, and all members united to Him and alive with His very divine life through His Holy Spirit are already "co-heirs" with Christ of heaven forever (Rm 8:17), yet there will be a "time" when all time as we know it will end and when "there is only Christ: he is everything and he is in everything" (Col 3:11).

Our Christian faith has maintained, down through history consistently and strongly, the teaching that Christ will come at the end of time to transform this universe by bringing it to its completion in and through Himself.

> And when everything is subjected to him, then the Son himself will be subject in his turn to the One who subjected all things to him, so that God may be all in all. (1 Co. 15:28)

God brings His creation to a consummation, for he does not create to destroy, but to fulfill. A true grasp of the resurrection of Jesus gives us a proper understanding of God's abiding love, not only for us human beings, but for His entire creation. The Christian message is this: "Yes, God loved the world so much that He gave His only Son so that everyone who believes in Him may not be lost, but may have eternal life" (Jn 3:16). It is not a restoration to an original state that existed in the garden of Eden and was lost through sin, but it is a bringing to fulfillment the tremendous potentiality locked in every atom of matter through God's uncreated energies of love in cooperation with the creative, loving actions of human beings.

To describe in a word the ultimate end of God's creation, Scripture, especially the New Testament writings, refers to it as the *parousia*. Jesus is already present in this material universe with His risen glory and power, bringing about victory over the dark powers of cosmic evil. But in a true sense, His victory will be perfect only at the end of time and this is the usual sense in which we use this term, *parousia*, or Christ's second and final coming. Christ will appear in all His glory

149

when His Body, the Church, with all its members, angels and saintly human beings, who will be the "contact" instruments of Christ risen to the material world, will manifest more perfectly than now in this "not yet condition," the fullness of Christ, the total Christ, the head, and His members. This will mean that the gospel will have been preached and lived throughout the entire universe.

A Harmony Among All God's Creatures

This is a most important teaching that is quite unique to Christianity. It confesses that we human beings have been meant by God to live in harmony with the entire material world. It professes the belief that God's redeeming love extends, not merely to the spiritual side of mankind, but also embraces the materiality of the whole cosmos. We in God's creative Word are all interconnected, angels, human beings and all the sub-human cosmos. We cannot be redeemed, unless the world that made us what we are is also brought into the same redemption. The Good News is that Jesus Christ is already here bringing about the kingdom of God in our lives and, through us, bringing it about in the entire world.

We can be sidetracked from the essential elements of this important teaching of the second coming of Christ, if we take too literally the scriptural images of life after death, as though they will happen exclusively at the end of our human history. To be concerned about how Jesus will look when He comes again to this earth in a cloud of glory to snatch us up with Him to live forever in glory can take us away from the true message of God and His true reality in our present existence. By focusing upon the *parousia* as an eschatological fulfillment that is dependent upon our daily living in the death-resurrection of Jesus Lord, we will be living this doctrine and, in the best way, we will prepare for His ultimate coming in glory.

Joseph Bonsirven, a noted New Testament scholar, describes this eschatological message of the Gospels:

The doctrine of the resurrection of the body on the last day is retained, but there is no description of the *Parousia*, or of the signs which will precede the Second Coming. Instead, the emphasis is placed on the element of present fulfillment: eternal life is present possession; the spiritual is already given to us; the Judgment itself is anticipated in the present and so is the Parousia.[1]

The End Of The World

Questions about the end of the world have always intrigued us. We are curious about what the world in the life to come will look like. St. Paul tells us not to speculate idly about what kind of body we will have in the life to come. Such questions are idle speculations and "stupid questions" (1 Co 15:36). The end of the world is not tied to some mathematical equation concerning the heat-death of the world that science can predict for us. It is tied intrinsically to our history as persons who make decisions to live in love or in fear and selfishness. The end of the world is tied, not merely to God's ultimate decree, but to our human ability to form free decisions as to the direction of this universe. Thus, we can never know when the fullness of this world will come and when the transformation of this material existence will move the cosmos into a new spiritual existence.

Jesus, in the apocalyptic discourses found in the three synoptic Gospels of Mark, Matthew and Luke, had much to say about the end of the world. He, or the authors of these Gospels, used the eschatological imagery already found in the prophets Isaiah, Ezekiel and Daniel, along with the apocryphal writings, such as the Books of Henoch, that were so popular from the 2nd century B.C. through the first century A.D. among the Jews of Palestine. Jesus Himself clearly

---

[1] Joseph Bonsirven, SJ, *Theology of the New Testament* (Westminster, MD: Newman Press, 1962), p. 148.

states, "But as for that day or hour, nobody knows it, neither the angels in heaven, nor the son, no one but the Father" (Mk 13:32).

The important scriptural message about the end of the world that Jesus leaves with us through the teaching of the Evangelists is that the end of the world is firmly and indissolubly linked to the person of Jesus Christ Who, as the Messiah, the Lord of the universe, will take the kingdom of God up with Him to share in His power and His glory. He has sovereignty over the entire world and this reign will be manifested at the end of the world, so that all nations can see that Jesus Christ is the Lord, the one to Whom power and dominion have been given by the Father to unite all things into a loving submission to God (1 Co 15:28).

The other message about the end of the world, as we have already indicated several times, is the urgency of vigilance in the *now* moment because the Son is already coming into His fullness through His loving members, who cooperate with Him to build His Body. He is hidden, but already bringing about the glorification of the universe. "Watch, be vigilant," is the message about the end of the world. But, it is also a message of joyful hope. *Maranatha!* is the hopeful expectancy that gives us courage in the dark night to await with joy the coming of the dawn of the full light of Christ as Lord. "Come, Lord Jesus" (1 Co 16:22). With great longing in our hearts we, too, are to go forth into our world and to unveil the hidden presence of the Risen Lord as we seek lovingly to serve each other and, therefore, to bring Christ to full maturity.

Final Judgment

The future final judgment of the world, passed by the Son of God, Jesus Christ, has also been an important belief in the Christian message about the end of the world. Jesus is seen in the eschatological discourse in Matthew's Gospel as gathering the entire world, "all the nations," into a final judgment and a sifting of those who will be "saved" and those who will be condemned.

> When the Son of man comes in his glory . . . before him will be gathered all the nations, and he will separate them one from another, as a shepherd separates the sheep from the goats . . . . Then the King will say to those at his right hand, "Come, O blessed of my Father, inherit the kingdom prepared for you from the foundation of the world."
> (Mt 25:31-34)

This is more than a static moment at the end of the world and more than a judgment on the particulars of our good and bad deeds done while on earth. It is in and through this judgment that God will establish the heavenly community, the ultimate state of His kingdom of heaven. When God manifests Himself in the fullness of Christ then every one of us will be exposed and seen in the light of Christ. Our identity will be seen in the degree to which we allow the love of Christ's Spirit to create us into our true selves in Him through our loving relationships with the other members of Christ's Body.

The consummation of the world will be a judgment. Those human beings, who have lived their Baptism through death to selfishness and in loving service to others, will enter into a life of intimate union with the Trinity and with all other angelic and human spirits and with the entire universe, that we could call the state of *heaven*. They will know that that state was theirs while they lived on this earth in love toward others. Others, who have encased themselves into self-centered love, will be judged to be only that. They will find that their earthly lives prepared them by their free choices to a limited view of reality. This is what we could call the state of *hell*.

It will be Christ Who, in a special manner, will be manifested as the Universal Judge. "He is the one ordained by God to be judge of the living and the dead" (Ac 10:42). This will be His crowning victory over sin and death and will be seen in the intimate union between the members of His Body, the angels and the saints, and their Head, Christ. Here, in the final judgment, we see the fullness of His Lordship exercised over the entire universe. Here we see the full meaning of His resurrection, and it carries with it a sharing of glory and power to all who have shared in His sufferings, death and resurrection to love others.

> You have been taught that, when we were baptized in Christ Jesus, we were baptized in his death; in other words, when we were baptized, we went into the tomb with him and joined him in death, so that as Christ was raised from the dead by the Father's glory, we too might live a new life (Rm 6:1-4).

The teaching about the final judgment is that, as we share in His sufferings through living in love toward others, so we are to share in His glory (Rm 8:17). The details of what it will mean in the final judgment to enter into the fullness of the resurrection and glory of Jesus Christ, to become heirs of God and co-heirs with Christ forever (Rm 8:17), can only remain in the hiddenness of expectant hope. "No eye has seen, nor ear heard, nor the heart of man conceived, what God has prepared for those who love him" (1 Co 2:9).

Final Glory

If we are guided by the experience of the resurrection of Jesus Christ in our present *now* of this earthly existence, we will see that we are already "becoming" a part of the total, glorified Christ. We have pointed out in the last chapter how the Eucharist, celebrated and lived by members of the Body of Christ, as they commemorate what He did by laying down His life as a sacrifice and a sacrament of love for all mankind, already brings us into union with the Trinity and with all members of the Church, both on earth, in glory (the angels and the saints) and in the state of purification.

As the resurrection of Jesus, Whom we receive in the Eucharist, describes how divinity and humanity came together in the oneness of His total person, so we can live in the hope that God has created each of us to become a vital part of the one Body of Christ. The Eucharist symbolizes, but also effects, the union between the Head and members, as Christ in His Spirit brings all creation into a "new creation." All creatures, we hope in Christ's Spirit, will share in God's eternal, trinitarian life by being a part of that Body. And that Body will be the source of praise and glory to Him, the Source of all life and beauty, as we live in the ultimate truth: "There is only Christ: he is everything and he is in everything" (Col 3:11).

But this final glory of the Body of Christ risen is being realized even now, as we learn to surrender ourselves in loving service to each other through the Spirit of the Risen Lord. The resurrection is a process of the coming into glory of the full Christ. This comes about gradually through the symbol of the cross and death, a symbol of continued purification and conversion away from dark egoism to embrace and live in the inner light of Jesus risen and living within us. Resurrection is a series of "yeses" to the dictates of Jesus' Spirit.

As we let go of our pseudo-control over our existence and independence from God and neighbor and our material world and "pass over" to a greater union in a loving *I-Thou* relationship in a larger *We* community, the Body of Christ, we are entering into the state of heaven, the state of oneness with Christ and His members. But this means that we become "reconcilers" with Christ of the entire world. God gave us this work of handing on this reconciliation (2 Co 5:18). We have the dignity, both in this earthly existence and in the life to come before the fullness of Christ's glory is manifested, by our service within the Body of Christ to extend the reconciliation by Christ of all things back to the Father.

A Continued Process of Transformation

Jesus Christ is now achieving the victory over cosmic evil through all His members on earth and those living in Him in eternal life. He is overcoming the forces of death, sin and chaos and is bringing about a gradual transfiguration of the entire creation of God. But this transfiguration process, since it is energized by God's very own uncreated energies of love living inside His alive-members, will always rest in the freshness of the love acquired and enjoyed in prayerful union with God and with the loving members of the Body of Christ.

The Christian view of our identity in the final glory is not the Jewish understanding of a glory that will exist only in the body of human beings left on this earth, who will profit from our loving actions, while we lived. The life of glory is both a sharing in the corporate fullness of the Body of Christ and a finding of one's unique, personal fullness as a living member of that Body of Christ, with special gifts developed through loving service toward others.

Love Ever Grows

St. Paul assures us that, in the life to come, all other things will pass away, except love. "Love does not come to an end" (1 Co 13:8). Resurrection and our entrance into the kingdom of God are always happening, even now, as we live in the Spirit's love. Heaven is where God is being recognized as present and active in His uncreated love energies. He calls us to respond to His love and to accept a share in the risen Body of Christ as we humbly seek to serve each other in building the Body of Christ.

Moreover, St. Paul assures us that healthy members come in love to aid the injured. Love grows in loving service. Resurrection is love in action. We are sharing in Christ's resurrection as we not only die to selfishness, but also as we live for Christ. And this means that we live in loving service to bring the Body of Christ to its full resurrection and glory.

156

The kingdom of heaven is the entrance into the resurrection of Christ as we discover God in His unique love for each person whom we encounter. This interaction begins in this earthly existence and continues in the life to come. As we positively allow the power of God in Christ Jesus through His ever-present gift of His Holy Spirit to interact in all of us, our power to love increases. We experience the resurrection of the Lord exerting His power of glory upon us. As we grow in love, the resurrectional power of Jesus becomes more powerful and transformative in our lives. The Body of Christ also grows more full of glory and power.

God is becoming God and Jesus Christ is becoming *the* resurrection, as we become living signs of the new creation by the love we allow to shine forth from our lives into the lives of others. We are daily destroying the temple with all its built-in idols, as we allow Jesus risen to bring about the fulfillment of His words: "Destroy this sanctuary, and in three days I will raise it up" (Jn 2:19).

To let go and live in the mystery of love is to touch the wounds of the Risen Lord and know that God is raising His Son to new power and glory by bringing greater oneness in love among the members in oneness with their Head, Jesus Christ, The miracle of the resurrection is happening at every moment of our daily life and in the existence we call heaven, as we are open to God's Word speaking in His creative acts of raising us up to new levels of sharing in His resurrectional, transforming love. This moment is always a new beginning, the first day of eternity. Heaven is growing and all this happens, as we members live death-resurrection in this present *now* moment. We can interpret the beautiful words, ". . . as long as we love one another, God will live in us and his love will be complete in us" (1 Jn 4:12), to mean "as long as we love one another, Christ is more completely being risen in power and glory."

We will always be part of a New Jerusalem that is being fashioned whenever members in Christ love one another. In joy and peace we can say *no* to Babylon and *yes* to the New

157

Jerusalem, God's new creation. Rooted in the human situation of God's creation, we live in love and, through service, we seek for that New City that awaits us and, yet, mysteriously is already here among us (Rv 21:3-7).

Eye Has Not Seen

What strange ideas most of us Christians have about heaven. We usually lock ourselves into earthly experiences of space and time and merely project the same experience into a time that has no limit and space, and is unlimited. Our sugary, self-centered ideas of heaven do not match up with God's revealed Word in Scripture. The essence of heaven is among "the things that no eye has seen and no ear has heard, things beyond the mind of man, all that God has prepared for those who love him" (1 Co 2:9). "Yes, the heavens are as high above earth as my ways are above your ways, my thoughts above your thoughts" (Is 55:9).

It is important that we ponder about heaven with clear and correct ideas for we will then be guided as to how we can now best live on earth. Heaven is no "place" to which we *go* after we are purified for a certain number of years or days and then pop out of purgatory and go over into heaven. It is the fruition of who we have become on earth in our forgetting of self and our living in loving union with God, our fellow human beings and all the other creatures of God. It is a question of the real world as God sees it.

When we strip away all our earthly imaginations about heaven as an objective place where we will be eternally happy without anymore suffering and turn to Scripture, we find heaven primarily to consist in relationships. We relate to God in joy, peace and complete fulfillment. We think of heaven and we should see God as the goal of all our earthly strivings. He is the complete reason for our existence. The idea of heaven stresses the fullness of our awareness that God is not only the beginning and end of all reality, but that He is *our* loving Father through Jesus Christ in their Spirit.

158

We have been driven by an inner force, a burning, passionate desire to know and lovingly serve God in the deepest intimacy. We were created out of God's trinitarian community of Father, Son and Holy Spirit to share intimately in that very life of God. He, Who is love (1 Jn 4:8), wants us to enter into that ongoing life of love of the Trinity.

We Shall Be In Christ

From Scripture, therefore, we see that heaven will first be the fulfillment of our life in Christ, which Baptism brought about as we were incorporated into his Body, the church. God, as a community or family, extends Himself outward in an eternal, loving movement of self-giving Persons. As revealed by the Incarnate Word of God, that community of life is given to us to share and enjoy in and through Christ and His Spirit. Heaven is the kingdom of God within us, whereby, incorporated into Christ, made really one with Him through His Spirit by an inner regeneration (Jn 3:3,5), we are able to live in the trinitarian community.

The central message of the preaching of Christ is about heaven and His making it possible through His Spirit that we might find God's community of the Trinity living within and around us. We become empowered by that Trinity to bring forth other living communities of one and many in the power of God's Spirit of love. God, as community, is already infinitely loving each one of us from within.

As we open up to His love and care for us, in and through Christ and His Spirit, we are commissioned, both in this earthly existence and in our continued life after death, to build the community of the Body of Christ. We live for others by laboring to build a social order grounded on justice and love, humility and meekness, respect for the oneness of all creatures in Christ and their uniqueness in His creation. As members of His Body, we will seek always to serve each other's uniquenesss in love.

Interpersonal Relationships Always Growing

Most theologians before Vatican II, in teaching about the essence of our eternal happiness in heaven, described this in static terms of our "seeing" God's essence in the *beatific vision*. Such static fixity was deemed the ultimate of God's perfection as perfect and immutable.

Christians today yawn before such seriousness, as theologians in the past battled among themselves to explain just how it was possible for us to see God "face-to-face" in the beatific vision. Our modern world explodes into such fresh and exciting richness that, to consider heaven in any static and immobile terms, has very little meaning today. Heaven as a place to which the "saved" go to gaze upon the essence of God through the beatific vision is being replaced by a more dynamic concept of a state of continued growth as God, angels and human beings lovingly interact to bring forth God's initial creation into ever-increasing beauty and harmony and unity in love.

Far from being the static "vision" of gazing upon three immobile Persons of the Trinity, the beatific vision can become for us a dynamic and exciting process of continued growth in love of God and of neighbor. Caught up within the very dialectic of the Godhead, eternally moving from *Silence* to *Speech*, from perfect repose and motionlessness, to sharing love in movement toward another we, too, live in the blissful tension of peaceful repose and movement toward others in love.

How exciting to think that heaven will be a state of continuous growth in loving "towardness" toward God and all His creatures, especially in loving service toward other human beings and not, after all, an "old folks' home"! St. Gregory of Nyssa of the 4th century describes true perfection in Heaven as "never to stop growing toward what is better and never to place any limit on perfection."[2] Grace, or the life of

---

[2] St. Gregory of Nyssa, *On Perfection*, tr. by V. W. Callahan in *Ascetica Works*; in series: *Fathers of the Church* (Wash., D.C., 1967), vol. 58, p. 122.

God within human beings and angels, both in this earthly life and in heaven, presupposes growth in accepting a loving relationship with God. And this means, above all, to accept the necessity of constantly moving in love toward God and neighbor.

If God is love and is limitless in His goodness and beauty and love toward us, our desire must also be limitless. The very unrest, the stretching forth to higher perfection, to greater union with the Trinity, is more than moving from one stage of perfection to another. It is more than a mere, static vision of God's beauty. God is eternally at rest yet He exists always in an outgoing motion of love to share Himself with others.

Continued Growth in Freedom

After the individual Christian has been purified in this life and in the life to come through the therapy of purgatory, he will stretch out ever more toward God, Who continually calls each person to "keep rising ever higher and higher, stretching with its desire for heavenly things to those that are before" (Ph 3:13), as St. Paul tells us . . . . And, thus, the soul moves ceaselessly upwards, always reviving its tension for its onward flight by means of the progress it has already realized. Indeed, it is only spiritual activity that nourishes its force by exercise; it does not slacken its tension by action, but rather increases it.[3]

Such spiritual growth, stretching in love toward greater union with the triune God and with other angels, saints and the whole human race, is what it means to be human. You become human, not only in the desiring, but by God's condescending giving of Himself always in newer and more amazing ways to you, who seek after Him with all your heart. "Happy are those who hunger and thirst for what is right: they will be satisfied" (Mt 5:6).

---

[3] St. Gregory of Nyssa, *Life of Moses*, cited in *From Glory to Glory*, tr. and ed. by J. Danielou and H. Musurillo (N.Y., 1961), p. 144.

This is the opinion of theologian Piet Schoonenberg, SJ, who insists on a growth process in the life to come:

> A certain growth also remains possible in the final fulfillment. Otherwise, we would perhaps cease to be human. Just as life constantly rediscovers itself from the past into the future, so we shall constantly rediscover our past and present in and from God in new and surprising ways.[4]

Can you, therefore, imagine that your purified, unselfish love for God will not enter into an ever-increasing, evolutionary growth in knowledge of God or loving surrender of self to serve God and neighbor? Heaven is that condition or state wherein you exercise the human freedom to give yourself to God and neighbor through loving service. Redemption should, perhaps, be better conceived of as, not a fixed state of beatific repose, but a growing process of discovering the love of God, both as manifested by his direct revelation of Himself to us in His trinitarian relationships and as manifested in His participated beauty in creation, especially in His angels and blessed human beings.

Love of Others

With the divine energies of God's love always surrounding you, both in this earthly existence and in the transformed world of heaven, and always calling you to respond to His Word, you reach the highest development by your continued cooperation to work with God's energetic presence in self-emptying love for others. As you cooperate with God's grace, you will come to meet God and glorify Him by your loving service toward other persons, both angels and human beings.

True prayer and sanctity, both in this earthly life and in

---

[4] Piet Schoonenberg, SJ, "I Believe in Eternal Life," in: *Concilium: Dogma, The Problem of Eschatology* (N.Y.: Paulist Press, 1969), P. 110.

heaven, must be measured exclusively by the degree of charity and humility possessed by the individual and shown in loving actions toward others. The love of God experienced in prayerful adoration before God "urges" you, to quote St. Paul's term, to go out from yourself in humble service to all who need more of God's love, of sharing more of God's beauty and perfection through your extension of His active love for others. Heaven can be no exception to the standard given us by Christ for life on earth, of measuring love for God by the love and service shown to your neighbor. You know whether God is in you by the love that you have for one another. True prayer is always begetting, becoming the other in greater unity of love that alone can be realized by humble service toward the other.

St. Therese of the Child Jesus beautifully expresses the importance of being love toward God and neighbor, which would apply equally as well in heaven:

> Love appeared to me to be the hinge for my vocation. Indeed I knew that the Church had a body composed of various members, but in this body the necessary and more noble member was not lacking; I knew that the Church had a heart and that such a heart appeared to be aflame with love. I knew that one love drove the members of the Church to action, that if this love were extinguished, the apostles would have proclaimed the Gospel no longer, the martyrs would have shed their blood no more. I saw and realized that love sets off the bounds of all vocations, that love is everything, that this same love embraces every time and place. In one word, that love is everlasting (*Autobiography*).

Heavenly Communion

As we have pointed out in dealing with the *parousia* or the end of time and of a material universe, when Jesus Christ will be manifested in His full glory, we long for a timeless time when there will be the condition of heaven and the possible condition of hell. The time of purifying those who in the eternal life after death needed to be healed of any remaining taints of selfishness will be over. There will only be the saints and angels living in loving union with the Trinity and with each other in their readiness to love all in order to share with others unto their fuller happiness the divine triune life. And there will also be the incomprehensible mystery of those who have died, hardened in a darkened world they themselves created out of repeated acts of selfish independence of God and neighbor.

Let us seek to imagine at least what communion among the saints and angels in heaven will mean. Let us keep always in mind the need we have to move always beyond the limitations of our earthly experiences when we think of heaven. Karl Rahner gives us this important caution: "It is *a priori* senseless to ask where heaven is, if by this 'where' we are to understand a location in our physical, spatial world."[5]

We cannot imagine what a spiritual body or a spiritualized person in glory will mean in being toward others who also are spiritualized. We can believe in that heavenly existence all fears will be replaced by love. Gone will be the aggressive attacks on others, now replaced by a Christ-like gentleness as you open up to receive God's diaphanous presence shining toward you, through the prism of each human and angelic spirit encountered. The Christ in you embraces the Christ in your neighbor and you respond with the excitement of new discoveries of God's beauty in your oneness in Christ. No longer is the other a stranger, a simple object "over there," separated from you. He or she becomes your brother or sister and you and they are vital parts of Christ. You discover your uniqueness as you live in the dynamic of Christ's Spirit of "passing-over" from yourself to lovingly

[5] Karl Rahner, *Theological Investigations* (Baltimore: Helicon Press, 1964), vol. 11, p. 215.

serve the other and, thus, build up the total Christ by every thought, word and action.

No longer will there be two commandments: to love God and then to love your neighbor. If you truly are loving God and experiencing His love for you, you will be loving God in all persons and experiencing His love as you accept their love. Each love relationship will be unique and God-revealing. Such love experienced will call out a new impulse to give yourself lovingly in service to others.

Through purification, Christ will have entered into all of your earthly experiences once your self-centeredness has yielded to Christ-centeredness. You will, therefore, be able to share your past experiences with others. All will be unto God's glory. Nothing will be merely "natural" or "secular." God will be "all in all" as you can share your experiences in education, travel, in human loves, in sufferings, and in discovering God's beauty in all human experiences, no matter how insignificant they may have appeared to you while you lived on earth.

All persons in Christ will develop even further talents and abilities in loving service. What would prevent Mozart and Beethoven from producing even more God-revealing music than they did on earth? The beautiful and famous saints, like the Apostles and the martyrs, and the unknown "little" saints, who served Christ and His Body in hidden fidelity and great love, will all vie with each other to be the humblest and most zealous to love and serve others. Everyone will be content with his or her charisms. In heaven, there will be no jealousy or competition, but only loving service.

How angels and human persons will intercommunicate in heaven has not been revealed to us by God. That is part of what awaits us. But we can truly believe that "communion of saints" means greater oneness in Christ's Body in intimate union with Him as their Head.

Heaven: A New Beginning of True Life

Heaven is not the end of our existence, our finally coming home to rest eternally. It is the beginning of true life, God's life which has already begun on this earth. It is like an onion made up of layer after layer and consists in nothing but circles of layers. To go deeper and deeper into God's love is to make each circle larger than the last.

It is a dance that starts even in this life, as we begin to love and dance in joyful harmony with other persons in true, godly love. An ever-widening circle of love extends outward to embrace other dancers. The dance goes on forever; new dancers join us as the circle of our love, which is one with the love of Christ in us, the Holy Spirit, extends itself to embrace the whole world of God's dancing creatures.

Our primary focus of activity will be to enjoy God and all His creatures in Him. This can have very little appeal to persons who on earth have never thirsted for God and have not drunk from the living waters of God's love. Rooted in God's being as the Source of our identity, we will explore the many ways God concretely loves us. We will discover, as we have also discovered in some limited way in this earthly life, His outpouring love, first, into our own life and in so many different ways.

We will be amazed as we discover the converging of all those love moments to allow us to enjoy God in this *now* eternal moment of love. As we know and love ourselves in God's tremendous and unique love for each of us, we will still see our love for ourselves, God and others needing development. In communion with the angels and saints, will we know and want to know facts about their lives, their experiences? Yes, but only in the measure that we wish lovingly to serve them through such knowledge and praise God for His active love in those experiences. There will be no place for idle curiosity stemming from pride and selfishness. We will relax and be honest without any need to protect our "interests" at the cost of true union in love with others. We will live according to St. Paul's injunction: "If we live by the truth and in love, we shall grow in all ways into Christ . . . . So the body grows until it has built itself up in love" (Ep 4:15-18).

We will see the secret happiness that we glimpsed on earth from time to time and will learn that the more we live to serve another in love, the more we receive God in that person. We give in service, not for any self-centered advantages, but only to draw out happiness in others. Heaven is truly a door (Rv 4:1) that opens before us so that we can humbly and joyfully enter into God's reality. And part of God's real world, as Jesus has revealed to us, is that God has created all things in and through His Son (Jn 1:3). Yet, we are called to be "co-creators" with Christ to evolve the created, material world in all its diversity and complexity into a oneness in Christ unto God's eternal praise and glory.

The Cosmic Christ

Christian doctrine holds a basic optimism toward God's material creation that He sees always as "good" (Gn 1:18). It teaches in apocalyptic imagery that Christ will come at the end of time to transform this material universe by bringing it to its completion in and through Himself. Just how this will be accomplished has not been revealed in detail. St. Paul writes, "We know that God was truly reconciling the world to himself in Christ" (2 Co 5:19). Each individual member of Christ has a role to play on this earth and in the glorious life to come in the reconciliation of the cosmos to Christ's power and rule. The Body of Christ will be filled up, not only with living human members submitted to Christ's reconciling power, but through their cooperation in relationship to the material world, the subhuman cosmos will lead in a mysterious way the created world back to the Father in Christ. "He has put all things under his feet, and made him, as the ruler of everything, the head of the Church, which is his body, the fullness of him who fills the whole creation" (Ep 1:22-23).

No longer will there be chaos, dissension, aversion of the created, subhuman world from God. The whole brute world will have reached its completion in being transfigured from its deformity, its "vanity," as Paul calls it, into a "renovated creation." Our world will not be annihilated, but transfigured. There will be a com-union of saints with the spiritualized world as the saints will cooperate to evolve that world into a manifestation of Christ's power and dominion even over the subhuman cosmos.

We are in need of recapturing the vision of St. Paul, St. John and the early Christians, especially the early Greek Fathers. They saw in Jesus Christ the *Alpha*, the beginning, in whom all things were created (Jn 1:2). They also saw Him as the *Omega*, the goal, the end toward which every finite creature was moving as toward a magnet that drew, by an active force of personalized love, all human beings, as well as the created world.

We Christians actively will work to move the created world from death and corruption, the wages of sin, to incorruptible life in Christ. Jesus Christ, vibrantly alive and inserted into the material world and working actively with our cooperation, is the key to true progress and the full meaning of this created cosmos. The whole creation, including human beings, who freely submit to the guidance of Jesus Christ, is to be brought into the glorification of God. Jesus Christ is *now* accomplishing this in the created universe. But its completion and fulfillment will be a part of heaven and our human cooperation to complete God's initial plan to create all things in His Word (Jn 1:2).

> Once everything has been brought into subjection
> to him, then the Son himself, in order that God
> may be everything to everyone, will be brought into
> subjection to the Father who subjected everything
> to him, in order that God may be everything to
> everyone and everything. (1 Co 15:28)

What About Hell?

It has always been a difficult subject to accept: the exis-

168

tence of hell as a place of eternal punishment created by God to obtain justice against those fallen angels and human beings who have not lived in love of God and neighbor. How can such a vindictive God be the same merciful and forgiving God who can never be but eternally and unchangingly a loving Father to all His children created in His Son's likeness? How can God build a fiery hell and punish millions for all eternity and then seemingly rejoice that His justice is being accomplished?

I know from experience in writing and preaching about hell that I set myself up to be misunderstood by those who read what I wish to present here. As long as we continue with the literal interpretation of the Old and New Testament views of hell as a material "place" filled with everlasting fire and brimstone and human and angelic spirits confined to that fiery prison for all eternity, we will have missed the essence of Christ's revelation about hell. We must see this powerful doctrine in the setting of relationships between God, whose mercy and love endure forever, and His created children.

If we, while on earth, continue to make choices based on selfishness, rather than self-sacrificing love, we will enter into a state of isolation, that destroys God's true life shared through authentic love for others. Hell is most real, but it is found in our hearts and not in some "place" below the earth. From God's side, He can never go against His nature, which is always to love us actively. Yet, from our human side, we can continuously make choices that separate us from God and the rest of His created world.

Thus, modern theologians holding this view do not deny the existence of hell, but rather they highlight its reality for those who freely set themselves up during their earthly existence to create their own world centered around their self-centeredness and independence from God and all other creatures. From the side of human and angelic spirits, who have freely chosen to live in selfishness and not in self-sacrificing love toward God and neighbor, there can be no liberation from the fires of internal frustration within their hearts to live in communion with God and all other creatures. What God can do for the "damned" in His uncreated energies of love and by the extension of His incarnate love by members of Christ's Body, who bring Christ's love to them, we cannot say with certainty.

This does not mean that God gives them another chance in the life to come or that surely all creatures will one day be saved from the fires of hell and come into salvation. This doctrine of *universalism* has been condemned consistently in early church councils as heretical. Jesus preached that, if human and angelic beings would not turn away from selfishenss and live in true love toward God and neighbor, there would be no exit out of hell. Once angels and human beings have freely determined themselves to a lifetime of selfishness and created a false world with themselves as the center instead of God, they individually cannot help themselves. They are "black holes" who have turned within and live in a world that is totally unreal, since it was not created as such by God.

God's Infinite Mercy

We must ever remain in the mystery of God's love and mercy, so powerfully revealed by the human actions of Jesus Christ, especially in His sufferings and death on the cross; we must never lose hope in what His love can accomplish. His love can do more than we could ever hope for. Yet, we cannot conclude that, therefore, God's love definitely will conquer the obstinacy of all resisting persons and hell will one day cease.

Wrapt in awe that God loves us actively and forever, regardless of our response to Him, we can say no more. But we can also believe that the same order of salvation as we can experience on this earth will continue in the life to come. Here God, through the living members of the Body of Christ, the Church, makes incarnate His great, self-sacrficing love

170

for all mankind through those who make up Christ's extended Body. God touches the sinful and unloving persons by those who are loving and in whom Christ lives, and loves the needy and destitute with His extended love, which He showed to all the sick and the sinful while He lived on earth.

Cannot God directly continue to reveal His immense and perfect love in the life to come as Jesus imaged that love on earth? On whose authority can we ever dictate to God what He must do and not do? Why must His love operate only until the time of our death? If God were to discontinue to love in an active, involving way every one of His creatures, would He be love by nature?

"Communion of saints" must also speak of God's love and mercy going out toward the needy in self-sacrificing, Godly-love precisely through the active caring of His loving saints. We have seen St. Paul's teaching, "Love does not come to an end" (1 Co 13:8). For the saints, heaven is where God is present. Yet, their love burns within them to share the goodness of God with others. Paul assures us that the healthy members of the body come to the aid of any injured or needy members. "If one part is hurt, all parts are hurt with it" (1 Co 12:26). In the Body of Christ, the healthy, saintly members come to the rescue of those who are injured. A sign of love is self-sacrificing service to the point of wanting to lay down one's life for the happiness of another (Jn 15:13).

Unveiling God's Love to the Needy

Who among all of God's creatures are more needy than those in the state of hell? The saints desire to be all things to all persons to win them to Christ, as Paul wanted to do. Why should the love of the saints in heaven be restricted and less self-sacrificing toward the forlorn and forsaken in hell than their love was toward the needy while they lived on earth?

True love always partakes somewhat in the madness of martyrdom. Christian martyrdom becomes self-emptying

171

love for the happiness of another only because the love of God in Christ has been revealed in the heart of such a loving Christ (Rm 5:5). This love of Christ transforms the individual Christian into a similar love. It binds the Christian into a union with Christ. The martyr becomes a healthy member, tied irrevocably to his Head, Jesus Christ, only by love poured out freely, even to the point of death, for others.

Can we imagine any saint in the state of heaven who would not wish to live in such a martyr's love toward the most pathetic and needy of persons? Would not such a saint wish a share in the sufferings and condemnation of Jesus on the cross unto death? H. Urs Von Balthasar dramatically interprets the theology of Georges Bernanos in terms of ultimate love of Christ in the mystic conquering him to the point of "folly" in order to lead others to Christ:

> As far as Bernanos is concerned, true mysticism "does not resemble that which we read in books." It consists simply in this: that one allows himself to be thrown out of all shelter, not only out of wordly shelters, but even far away out of that supernatural security of the life of faith, as guaranteed by the Church herself. The true mystic is a man who lets himself be cast down into the abyss, where he is tossed about in all directions, in a kind of darkness where there is no distinction between up and down, to be forsaken by the Father is to be delivered into the hands of Satan.[6]

In heaven, the saints, even though they know they can never be damned because of their love for Christ, still know that their love must stretch itself to such heights of "folly" because of the great love unto folly that they have experienced from Jesus Christ. The more one is raised to this life in Christ, the more such a person enters into communion with

---

[6] H. Urs von Balthasar, *Le Chrétien Bernanos* (Paris: Seuil, 1963), pp. 160-161.

all other human beings and the entire created world. There develops within such a person a genuine sense of being one with the whole world, created by God and loved by God as very good.

One is open and ready to give of oneself to the whole world, but in a special way to those most destitute and ignorant of God's perfect love for them in Christ Jesus. They not only live in the hope that all persons will come to know Jesus Christ as the Father's gift, but that they can become the instruments whereby God actively brings His life-giving love to the needy. Jesus Christ is now achieving the victory over cosmic evils through all His members.

Hell is very real from the viewpoint of the person living in selfishness. But it is totally beyond our imagination what God can do through His saints, who, in true Christian hope and love, strain to stretch out to those groaning in travail. It has not been revealed how this interaction takes place, but it is of the essence of what *communion of saints* means.

The holy ones of God, who have understood St. Paul when he wrote, ". . . the only thing that counts is not what human beings want or try to do, but the mercy of God" (Rm 9:16), share in the pain of the Good Shepherd who searches for His lost sheep, not only on this earth, but in the farthest reaches of hell.

Reconciling The Disunited

To this role of cooperating with Christ to reconcile the disunited into unity through the love of Christ's Spirit, God calls all the healthy members in the Body of His Son. The question is not theirs to ask: "Will eventually all in hell accept God's love in Christ Jesus? Will all God's creation be reconciled into a perfect oneness?" Theirs is only to show the love and mercy of Christ toward all who suffer and lie in darkness. Theirs is to be the light of Christ to the blind. Theirs is to release the love of God in Jesus Christ through their love toward the most despicable and forsaken beings. For they know that Heaven is a state of happiness in God's love that is measured by death to self and a rising with Christ to love and serve the needy. Such love grows on sacrifice and self-giving. Greater union with Christ and eternal happiness in Heaven come by service to the poor. "I tell you solemnly, insofar as you did this to one of the least of these brothers of mine, you did it to me" (Mt 25:40).

Heaven and hell cannot be separated, as though they are two different places, because love breaks down all barriers of communication and builds reconciliation or loving union. *Communion of saints* is much more than the teaching of the Church that saints can intercede for the needy. It is the summary of the Christian life that God needs those transformed into healthy members of the Body of Christ to extend divine life to those who have not yet opened themselves to receive God's gift of triune life. We are all called and destined by God to live in loving union in Christ and with all God's creatures, especially with all His angels and human children made by the triune God, according to Christ's image and likeness.

St. Paul's summary is a fitting conclusion to these insights about the doctrine of the communion of saints:

> And for anyone who is in Christ, there is a new creation; the old creation has gone, and now the new one is here. It is all God's work. It was God who reconciled us to himself through Christ and gave us the work of handing on this reconciliation. In other words, God in Christ was reconciling the world to himself, not holding men's faults against them, and he has entrusted to us the news that they are reconciled. So we are ambassadors for Christ; it is as though God were appealing through us, and the appeal that we make in Christ's name is: be reconciled to God. For our sake, God made the Sinless One into sin, so that in him we might become the goodness of God. (2 Co 5:17-21)

Appendix

Spiritism And Devil Possession

We have already developed at some length in the preceding chapters the principle of a good and salutary "spiritism." God has ordered the completion of His creation to be brought about by the free-will cooperation in loving service by His most highly-endowed intellectual creatures, angelic spirits and human beings. Therefore, there exists a healthy *spiritism* in which we are encouraged by God's revelation and taught by the church from earliest times to make prayerful contact with God's angels and saints, our departed loved ones, to seek their intercession and loving help in our many earthly needs. This teaching and practice are founded in Jesus' teaching of the Church as an organic life in Him, Who is the Head, and the members, living in Him through God's grace, forming one Body with all others alive in Christ by the same divine elevation.

But there exists in all religions, and Christianity is no exception, a false *spiritism*. Although this book deals primarily and positively with the correct communion of, and with, the saints, I believe it is worth an appendix to develop a proper teaching on a false spiritism and devil possession, since it is usually difficult to find an adequate modern presentation on this topic, in spite of a rather popular, but morbid interest in contacting "spirits" in order to gain knowledge of the future or power or riches in a selfish manner.

Occultism

All human beings throughout the ages have been intrigued by the unknown forces that seemingly shape their lives. They have always wanted the power to know what lay ahead of them in the future and, above all, they have wanted the power to control such forces for their own well-being.

When you hear the word *occultism*, what ideas do you associate with it? Some, conservative Christian fundamentalists, would give the name *occult* to all forms of fortune-telling, magic, spiritism. A few would classify clairvoyance, telepathy, hypnotism, any form of divinization, or ESP (extrasensory perception) under *occultism* and confine such to the kingdom of Satan.

To those of a broader perspective, occultism is their way of describing merely the whole world of the unknown, of what has not yet been brought under scientific study. Dr. J. B. Rhine, well known for his parapsychological work at Duke University, describes it: "Occultism usually connotes unorthodox, mysterious beliefs and obscure magical practices, implying the presence of some principle outside the scope of the natural world, inaccessible to scientific study."[1]

Occultism is not necessarily an evil. It embraces all phenomena which science has not yet thoroughly explored and classified according to universal laws. Until recently, the occult concerned areas of extraordinary human powers in the psychic field. Most occult practices are linked with the mystery of mind over matter, employing such powers as clairvoy-

---

[1] J. B. Rhine, "Occultism," in, *The Encyclopedia Americana*, vol. 20 (NY., 1957), p. 609.

ance, telepathy, precognition and other forms of ESP. Now, psychology and the new science of parapsychology are studying such "occult" powers. Thus, science is constantly invading the area of the occult to research and bring to light what formerly was considered as mysterious and unknown.

Magic

In spite of the efforts of science to classify and understand the traditional areas assigned to the occult, in the past decade we have witnesed a tremendous surge of interest in and actual practice of the occult as occult, not scientific inquiry.

To understand occultism, we need to understand its chief constitutive element, i.e., magic. Magic, along with religion and science, has always been a common response to the mysteries of life. Evidently, we are not dealing here with parlor tricks or the theatrical magic which is a form of entertainment, using sleight-of-hand, rapid movements and mechanical constructions to create a false illusion to prove over and over that the hand is quicker than the eye.

Etymologically, the term "magic" is derived from the Greek word *mageia* and the Latin *megia* to refer to the occult teachings and practices of the Persian Magi. Magic covers a great panoply of practices, especially among primitive peoples, from actions to produce an abundance of food and drink, rain, disaster upon one's enemies, or conquest of a person whom one sexually desires, through love potions, etc. Magic is a symbolic mode of ritual, both verbal and nonverbal, designed to obtain powers and favors from a personal or impersonal power found inside of nature that are beyond man's own doing.

White Magic

According to its aims or the effects desired, magic in its long history has been classified as productive, protective and destructive. Sometimes magic designed for benevolent effects is called *"white magic."* *"Black magic"* seeks a destructive power, usually through an appeal to demons of evil. To some degree, science grew out of the struggles between magicians and priests. Astronomy developed from astrology, chemistry from alchemy and medicine from witch doctors or healing ministers of religion.

The Bible On Magic

Many conservative Christians condemn any form of psychic experience as being a part of magic which they find to have been roundly condemned on the pages of the Bible. We read in the Old Testament:

> There must never be anyone among you, who makes his son or daughter pass through fire, who practices divination, who is soothsayer, augur or sorcerer, who uses charms, consults ghosts or spirits, or calls up the dead. For the man who does these things is detestable to Yahweh, your God; it is because of these detestable practices that Yahweh, your God, is driving these nations before you. (Dt 18:10-12)

The chosen people of God were not to seek guidance in any other way than in prayerful communication with God. Holy Scripture forbids man to seek hidden knowledge of the future through any preternatural or demonic power. King Saul violated the first commandment (Ex 20:3,5) by consulting the witch of Endor (1 S 28) and for this reason God slew him (1 Ch 10:13-14).

It is clear that the Bible is against magic in any form that seeks power and knowledge from any source but God. But it is naive for fundamentalists to build up a sweeping condemnation against all occult forms, including psychic manifestations, from a few texts that pitted divination through magicians or by necromancy (consulting the departed spirits

178

for knowledge or power). Many of these condemnations in the Old Testament were to prevent any other religious force from functioning outside of the Israelite religious system.

Satanism

Occultism, therefore, admits of a wide variety of experiences. Great discernment is needed to determine, not only the source of the given power, but also the goal of the individual who experiences such power. All religions, especially Judaism and Christianity, have attributed to devils, fallen angelic spirits, hidden powers on the physical, psychic and spiritual planes.

Man's reactions to demonic attacks have been of a dual nature. History has shown that in all times there have been certain individuals, typified by Goethe's *Faust*, who actually have worshipped Satan, the leader of all evil demons, in order to gain hidden powers unpossessed by ordinary human beings. Other human beings have not actively invited Satan to take over in a worshipful self-surrender, yet they experience unwillingly Satan's powers through *possession* or *obsession*.

First, a word about *Satanism* as a willing act of worship to gain power. *Spiritism* is a related term that is often used to describe any occult contact with spirits, especially evil ones. Such practices can be found in all primitive races, mixed with a view of *animism*, i.e., that all of nature is animated for good or evil by spirits whose favors can be won or lost. Burial rites and religious practices to ward off bad spirits from the departed or the living are found in such cultures. A well-known ritual for cursing someone and placing the "evil eye" on an enemy still persists in West Indian *voodooism* that has found a place among Caribbean immigrants to American cities and into our American movies and books.

Satanism, or worship of Satan as the prince of evil spirits to gain power, is rooted in the Old and New Testament teachings about Satan as a fallen, angelic spirit. He tempts

179

human beings to sin, seeking to thwart God's plan of restoring the universe through the mediation of Jesus Christ.

Witchcraft

Witchcraft refers to the practice of the arts of magic to obtain preternatural powers through association with devils such as an appeal to evil spirits to inflict harm on persons, to communicate with the dead or to foretell future events. The Middle Ages saw not only a negative attitude on the part of church officials toward witchcraft but, urged on by a militancy that made a mockery of the non-violence taught by Jesus Christ, some church leaders aggressively attacked witches, or those thought to be witches, in order to exterminate such influence from Europe.

Modern Witchcraft

When society becomes confused about norms and methods to attain meaningful aims in life, modern man and woman tend to resort to some form of retreat into archaic, secured positions, or of ritualism or new forms of innovation or, finally, simply of forms of destructive rebellion. So it is no surprise that witchcraft with its "old religion" rituals is attracting more practitioners today in England and America than at any time since the Reformation.

One gross form of a return to submission to Satan through archaic symbols and rituals in order to gain release of sexual energy, to vent anger, lust, greed, pride, vengeance is Anton LaVey's Church of Satan in San Francisco. From his Satanic Bible, published in 1970, we can see an out-and-out attempt to fashion a religion in worship of Satan to gain in return any power that his followers seek.

A more nuanced and sophisticated "new" religion is the Process Church of the Final Judgment, founded in London in 1963 by youths of college age. It avoids the grossness and crude spectacularism of LaVey. Satan and Lucifer are classi-

180

fied along with Jehovah as the three gods of the universe. But Satan is more often a form of psychological interpretation of the dark and evil forces at work within each human person and in the world through social relationships.

Devil Possession

Occultism as primarily connected with devil possession received internal acceptance by the millions who viewed the film, *The Exorcist*. Movies, TV, a flood of horror books and heavy rock music, have brought the public to a new interest in devil possession, creating a *demonomania*.[2]

Also, the rapid spread of Pentecostalism has brought devil deliverance down to the common prayer meeting where devils are ejected on command through faith in the power of Jesus' name. Much confusion on this topic is found everywhere. Above all, some pastoral norms, based on long centuries of prudence in dealing with this subject and fortified by new finds in modern psychology, must be given.

Devil *oppression* is the state in which a person experiences normal attacks from evil spirits but in an external fashion. This is described in the New Testament as the common attack by the evil one against all Christians.

---

[2] Some suggested books on varying views are the following: Martin Ebon, *The Devil's Bride. Exorcism: Past and Present* (N.Y.: Harper & Row, 1974; Ebon, *Exorcism: Fact and Fiction* (N.Y.: Signet Books, 1963; Christopher Neil-Smith, *The Exorcist and the Possessed* (St. Ives, Cornwall, England: James Pike Ltd., 1974); T. K. Oesterreich, *Obsession and Possession by Spirits Both Good and Evil* (Chicago, IL: The de-Laurence, 1935); Dom Robert Petitpierre, ed., *Exorcism: The Findings of a Commission* (London: S.P.C.K., 1972); John Richards, *But Deliver Us From Evil. An Introduction to the Demonic Dimension in Pastoral Care* (London: Darton, Longman and Todd, 1974); Adolph Rodewyk, SJ, *Possessed by Satan. The Church's Teaching on the Devil. Possession and Exorcism*, tr by M. Ebon (Garden City, N.Y.: Doubleday and Co., 1975); Richard Woods, *The Devil* (Chicago: The Thomas More Press, 1973).

Be calm, but vigilant, because your enemy, the devil, is prowling around like a roaring lion, looking for someone to eat. Stand up to him, strong in faith and in the knowledge that your brothers all over the world are suffering the same things.

Theologians distinguish between devil "possession" and obsession. Both words have Latin roots and compare them to a city under attack by an enemy. *Possessio* means that the enemy, in this case, the Devil, has conquered the city and is in control of it from its internal strongholds. *Obsessio* means that the enemy has the city under siege and is able, by external assaults, to create several disturbances and chaos within the city. A. Winklhofer thus defines the assaults of evil spirits in a threefold manner. *Circumsessio* is an intensive siege of the person aimed at harming him and preventing him from fulfilling aims, but without actual control of the human being's organism.

Obsessio is a condition during which the demon, taking control of the person by living within him, uses his bodily organs, torments him and often provides him with extraordinary powers. This is more than what modern psychology terms "obsession," a neurotic condition with an emotional over-involvement with a particular act or idea. This is an actual entering into the person by the demon, but without suspending completely free will.

Possession is the state in which the person is a completely helpless object of demonic misuse of his sensory faculties, while his freedom is either nearly or totally suspended.

In true possession (and I do not wish to pass judgment on how frequently this happens) the devil dwells in the body, affecting the psychic and spiritual faculties of a man through a strong control over the bodily senses and imagination so that one's intellect and will can be held in abeyance or paralyzed. Cases of diabolic possession are mentioned in Mt 4:24; 8:28; 9:32.

Need For Caution And Discretion

The Roman Catholic Church has exercised extreme caution in discerning true possession from neurotic states and in using its God-given powers of *exorcism* through properly delegated exorcists, clergy of tested-holiness and wisdom. Because the line separating certain forms of neurosis from devil-possession is very thin, the Roman Ritual gives certain signs and precautions along with the rite of exorcism. As psychology deepens its knowledge of neurosis, what earlier centuries attributed to devil-possession now is often explained in terms of psychology.

Rev. Juan B. Cortes, SJ, Professor of Psychology at Georgetown University, believes *demon* is a pre-scientific word for what we call today a "complex" or an emotional conflict. He believes that the bizarre symptoms of demonic possession: throwing oneself about, uncontrollable cursing, violence, strange marks on the skin, can all be explained as those of certain brain and nervous disorders.[3] For this reason, the Church is slow in allowing an official exorcism to be conducted and only after great discernment.

In its discerning of a case of true possession, the Church gives some principal signs: 1. Sudden knowledge of foreign languages with a sudden capability of reading, writing or singing beyond a person's normal ability; 2. When he can converse on higher subjects of which he/she has had no previous knowledge; 3. When one reveals knowledge of secret things which only demons, no humans, could know, e.g., knowledge of hidden sins; 4. If an individual is unable to be kept from talking; 5. When he/she is unable to execute the command of calling upon God, Jesus, or the saints or when such a subject is unable to utter pious prayers; 6. When the person is frightened, pained or restless during the use of rel-

---

[3] Cited by William V. Rauscher with Allen Spraggett, *In The Spiritual Frontier* (Garden City, N.Y.: Doubleday and Co ., 1975) p. 155.

ics, the crucifix, a consecrated candle or holy water; 7. When one cannot bear the ritual of exorcism itself.[4]

Some Pastoral Guidelines For Deliverance

1. The first principle that we must hold onto with firmness and act upon is the conviction that Jesus Christ still heals, but He does so through the ministry of human beings who call upon His healing power. Jesus went about healing all the broken in body, soul and spirit who believed in His saving power (Mt 4:23-24; 9:35; 10:1). He gave this power to His disciples who extended this down through the centuries through the Church. We must first believe that Jesus is still alive and living in His members, the Church, and that He truly wants to save us, to heal us and to bring us into total health of mind and body by freeing us from all forms of brokenness and enslavement to diabolic, negative forces within us and our communities. We Christians have this God-given power to the degree that we are healed of our own demonic possession of self-centeredness. As we place Jesus Christ as our center, so we can go forth and be an instrument of delivering others from any force that holds them in bondage.

2. In dealing with deliverance we must realize that we are dealing with mytho-poetic imagery that goes beyond objectivization of rational language. It is difficult for most Westerners who have lost the ability to live with symbols, above all, in their religious lives, to speak of devils and refrain exclusively from objectivizing such into personalized fallen angels.

From our Christian faith we hold the possibility of such personalized spirits powerfully attacking us and even gaining control of our members and our intellect and will. And yet we must be ready to learn from psychologists not to attribute all mental derangement to the activity of such objec-

---

[4] Cited by Adolf Rodewyk, op. cit., p. 66.

tive demons, but to admit in the concept of *demonic* other forces that go much beyond the mere presence of demons.

How to use the demon imagery as Jesus did to refer both to activities of evil spirits and to physical and mental sicknesses without trivializing the immense reality of sin and evil in the person of a demon requires much study, both of the use of myths and of what psychologists can teach us.

3. Persons called to a ministry of healing, not out of an aggressive desire for power and fame, but out of a loving compassion for the broken ones of this world as Jesus did, must never attribute naively every physical and psychic evil to the direct activity of evil spirits. Such simple reduction creates havoc among highly suggestible persons and leaves them with a mental picture of an infestating devil. Such simplicity removes the struggle from the person seeking healing and fills him or her with the magical impression that what took years to develop can be magically healed instantaneously without any change in his or her moral life because now Jesus has driven out the evil spirit.

4. All Christians, through the faith, hope and love that they have received in their Baptism, have the power to apply the authority of Jesus Risen to the brokenness in their own personal lives and to intercede that Jesus may come into the lives of others for whom they pray and to whom they bring healing. This can often be done in silence. If it is done in praying over anyone, there must be a discernment to recognize what forces are at work in such needed deliverance.

5. Such discernment, in cases of serious obsession, should be done by holy and wise persons in a group in prayer. It is most dangerous for the individual healer, as well as for the one needing deliverance, to undertake such a task alone.

6. In the case that such a group of healers commands, rebukes and threatens evil spirits, in the name of Jesus, discernment must be made as to how they consider the evil spirits present and how will the one seeking deliverance interpret the mythosymbolic demon imagery. One of the great

deceits of evil spirits is to create the impression that they possess tremendous powers. By accentuating the personalized presence of such evil spirits, the focus in healing and in deliverance can readily be taken away from the power of God working through the Risen Jesus. We can learn from the lives of the saints who placed all their trust in the indwelling presence of God. "Let us keep our eyes fixed on Jesus, who inspires and perfects our faith" (Heb 12:2).

7. In praying over persons for deliverance, such action should be a part of a total healing. There should be a prayer for the in-filling of the Holy Spirit and, where it is possible, the use of the sacraments of Reconciliation, Eucharist and Anointing of the Sick. There should be a loving community that continues to support the one seeking deliverance with prayers and love. The one prayed over must see the healing process as a continued surrender to the powerful love of the Indwelling Trinity living within him or her.

8. If any strange phenomena occur while praying over a person for healing, especially if these phenomena manifest themselves in compulsive action in the physical order of voices, screams, physical convulsions, etc., such a person should be withdrawn from the gaze of others and brought into a quiet place where a team of prudent and solidly-grounded-in-faith persons can undergo a period of discernment of how to be most effective as a healing, loving and caring team to that person.

9. What should be avoided in such healing and deliverance services is a large gathering where devils are "coughed" up on signal by a powerful "deliverer." Such sessions soon end in hysteria and do untold damage to the mentally disturbed. Persons open to the power of suggestion can easily fall into the "contagion" of possession by witnessing a deliverance where too much accent is placed on the objective presence of a devil within the sick person. Praying over such disturbed persons should be done privately, in a prayerful context where Jesus Christ is exalted and not much show is given to devils. When physical manifestations begin, like

186

screaming, bodily writhing, cursing of Jesus Christ, foaming at the mouth and rolling on the floor, the individual should be removed from the crowd context and a few deeply prayerful persons should minister to that person without histrionics and any fearful accentuation of the presence of devils.

10. If there is a case that might come under possession and call for an exorcism, the pastor should be notified who, in turn, should be in touch with the local bishop. Here we see a most important need in dioceses of having some religious expert in the history of exorcism and in the ability to pray over such advanced cases of possession according to the norms and prayers set down in the *Roman Ritual*. Such cases will indeed be very rare, but at least when they occur, they should be handled with the authority of the bishop and his continued knowledge, so as to withdraw such a case from the hands of less prudent and qualified persons.

Conclusion

The point of this teaching on deliverance has primarily been to show that Jesus Christ desires that we, as persons healed of our broken, demonic dark sides, go forth in the paschal hope of His victory over the powers of sin and death to be a caring, loving presence of Jesus Christ to those who still are in bondage to the evil forces around and within them. Deliverance is a vital part of healing and is open to all Christians who believe in the victory of Jesus over sin and death.

But, as we have pointed out, deliverance language, rooted in the demon imagery of the New Testament and ritual prayers of the Church for the deliverance, tends to polarize those who approach this topic. Those of a more scientific bent tend to reduce all demonic forces only to mental aberrations while strongly denying the existence of spirits, both good and evil. Those of a more literal interpretation of Scripture tend to ignore the findings of psychology and move toward *demonomania*. They ignore secondary causes and credit all evil to the direct influence of evil spirits.

Through sciences, especially those that deal with the workings of the human psyche, and through biblical exegesis, we are fortunate today to see deliverance from a larger perspective. As we listen in love to what the Holy Spirit is teaching us about the forces of evil operating on the societal, as well as on the personal levels, we can move away from a literal and exclusive understanding of objective evil demons as the sole instigators of evil. We can, and should, by faith accept the evil influences of such spirits of darkness. But we will avoid the trap that feeds into greater evil by blaming all evils upon devils.

This teaching is offered as a preliminary presentation that hopefully will stimulate more comprehensive studies. Through solid teachings on this important subject of deliverance, many unnecessary evils will be avoided or lessened through a naive literalism of demons in praying for healing. But, above all, we Christians will have discovered the true theological focus that alone can release the full healing power of Jesus Christ within His Church to heal the broken ones of this world. We will learn to act with confidence in His power working within us to reconcile the world to Him. Rooted in Him and His resurrectional life, we can build up His Body to its full measure.

This is the vision of deliverance as a cosmic reconciliation that St. Paul gives us, not because we fear the powers of devils, but that we are rooted in Jesus Christ, Who calls us to be His reconcilers of a world that is in bondage, but is groaning in travail to be released.

> If then any man is in Christ, he is a new creature: the former things have passed away; behold, they are made new! But all things are from God, Who has reconciled us to Himself through Christ and has given to us the ministry of reconciliation. For God was truly in Christ, reconciling the world to Himself by reckoning against men their sins and by entrusting to us the message of reconciliation. On behalf of Christ, therefore, we are acting as ambas-

sadors, God, as it were, appealing through us. We exhort you, for Christ's sake, be reconciled to God. For our sakes, He made Him to be sin Who knew nothing of sin, so that in Him we might become the justice of God. (2 Co 5:17-21)

Necromancy

We come now to the topic of calling upon deceased human persons, usually in an attempt to obtain some knowledge of the future or some riches or power. This conjuration of the spirits of the dead to reveal the future or to influence the course of events is called *necromancy*. The Old Testament forbids necromancy (Lv 19:31). The normal form of conjuring up the dead human spirits is the *seance*. This is a spiritualist meeting to receive communications from the spirits of the dead. Contact is established with the dead through a spiritual medium.

The medium is supposed to possess extraordinary psychic powers to make contact with the dead and help those interested to uncover future events. Bishop James Pike, the controversial Episcopalian bishop, before his tragic death in the desert near the Dead Sea, stirred up much interest through his TV appearance and his account in his book, *The Other Side*, by his communications with his son, Jim, who had committed suicide. The mediums he used to make contact were Mrs. Ena Twigg, a famous English psychic, and Arthur Ford, one of the more noted American psychics and founder of *Spiritual Frontiers Fellowship*.

The traditional teaching of the Catholic Church has always been "hands off" seances and such communications through mediums. Father Bernard Häring gives us sound advice:

> To accept the authentic spiritualistic interpretation of the spiritualistic phenomena as actually due to the presence of the spirits of the departed is superstition. God in His all-wise providence will not per-

mit the souls of the dead to be forced to appear before us at the beck and call of such disedifying individuals as the mediums usually are.[5]

Reincarnation

One connecting topic of universal interest in all cultures and in all times is that of reincarnation. Let us examine this as a transitional topic from occultism to parapsychology. Reincarnation is the teaching that, after death, the soul passes into the body of another human being, animal, or even into a plant or inanimate object. It has been also termed transmigration of souls, or *metempsychosis*, and was taught by Pythagoras and Plato, certain Gnostic schools, including many modern Hindus and Buddhists, theosophists, Mormons, and followers of Edgar Cayce.

Briefly, such a teaching arises from a fundamental belief that in man the soul is not only distinct, but can be separated from the body, especially at death. Even in this life, many human beings have a distinct sense of *déjà vu*, of having already seen certain scenes or lived through certain experiences as though they come from deeply lodged remembrances from former lives. One main reason for the positing of such a view is to explain why the good suffer and the wicked prosper. *Karma* is considered a law among those who hold reincarnation that maintains that all of the good or evil effects accumulated during one's life have to be lived through in successive rebirths called *samsara*. Only when one fulfills all the required karma is he finally released from the transmigration process and reaches the state of *nirvana* or blissful oneness with the Universal One.

Today, hypnosis, drug experiences and deep transcendental meditation have opened up the unconscious of many persons to give them the impression that they possess gen-

---

[5] Fr. Bernard Häring, *The Law of Christ*, vol. 2, p. 228.

uine knowledge of a former existence. Edgar Cayce, one of the most remarkable American clairvoyants and healers (1877-1945), in his many trances told his audiences about his past lives, but also revealed knowledge from the former lives of those who sought such information.

A more scientific document of research was done by Dr. Ian Stevenson, M.D., Professor of Psychiatry at the University of Virginia.[6] He selects out of some two hundred reported cases of reincarnation, twenty, and gives a thorough documentation. His conclusions center around children of between two and four years old who begin to describe events and people in a previous existence. He concludes that reincarnation occurs all the time, but memory of previous existences is rare, happening most frequently when the death was violent. Spirits seem to be able to choose somewhat their next reincarnation. Such cases of reincarnational recall occur mostly among people who already accept the idea of reincarnation, especially in India and other Hindu and Buddhist countries.

A Christian View

C. G. Jung and other psychologists have indicated the collective unconscious and the power of the unconscious to store up and even evoke experiences that are hidden from the normal flow of consciousness. At any rate, the whole problem of reincarnation is an intriguing area for much more scientific investigation. For the Christian, I believe, the common meaning of reincarnation cannot be held. That God has created us mere spirits that migrate in and out of various bodies with the Absolute has been condemned by the Church against the Origenists of the 6th century in the Second Council of Constantinople (553), in its anathemas against the *apokatastasis* doctrine of Origen. Such a teaching would guar-

---

[6] Ian Stevenson, *Twenty Cases Suggestive of Reincarnation* (Surrey, England: M. C. Petro, 1958).

antee final salvation to all with the eventual bankruptcy of hell.

God creates a human person, not merely a spirit or a soul. The body is a unique part of a total being. The whole person is the object of God's love: body, soul and spirit. To believe in a series of reincarnations on such tenuous recall of a few documented cases against the clear guidance of Scripture and its interpretative teaching by the Church down through the centuries would be a great error. The basic Christian doctrine of the resurrection of the body would negate any transmigration theory of body to body.

A Christian could certainly hold a type of evolving life into greater consciousness in the life to come, reaching ever new levels of spiritualizing the body, soul and spirit relationships without, however, the spirit returning back to a terrestrial existence through a material rebirth in a body. The constant teaching of the Church, both East and West, about purgatory as a therapy to be undergone in a progressive process after death, along with the Church's teaching on the communion of saints influencing both the living and the departed by their interacting love, would hold out an exciting possibility in the life to come of a process of constant upward growth, of a series of "reincarnations" into more perfect body (spiritualized), soul and spirit relationships through a purification of selfishness and an openness to accept love from other, more perfected beings.

Discover answers. . .

. . . in LIVING FLAME PRESS books

Today's Christians have many questions to ask — questions on prayer, spiritual growth, suffering, unity, living as a Christian in today's turbulent society. Living Flame Press offers some answers, bringing you books by such prominent authors as George A. Maloney writing on spirituality, David E. Rosage on prayer and meditation, Robert Lauder on the challenge of Christian living, and many others.

Whatever road you travel towards spiritual growth, Living Flame Press has something to help you on the way, including Robert Wild for charismatic spirituality, John Randall for the seeker in Scripture, René Voillaume for Eucharistic devotion.

We've remembered the children too, with the popular *Noah and the Ark* and others on our expanding list.

Send for our free catalog and see how Living Flame Press can answer your questions.

....

To: Living Flame Press, 325 Rabro Drive, Hauppauge, NY 11788 (Tel. 516 348-5251)

I want to discover Christian answers! Please send me your free catalog.

Name..

Address ....

Town ....Zip ....

FAMILY SPIRITUALITY
Fr. Gene Geromel

The tensions and temptations of life in our modern
world are tearing at the very fabric of the family unit.
This book offers the Christian family solace and
strength. The author explains how the family as an en-
tity is, in fact, the vehicle by which its individual members can achieve a deeper relationship with God. The
author is an Episcopal priest with a family of his own,
and speaks with first-hand knowledge of family as the
way to God.

ISBN: 0-914544-67-5 $4.95

PRAYING WITH MARY
Msgr. David E. Rosage

This beautiful book offers twenty-four short meditations on key events in the life of our Blessed Mother.
Many readers have commented that *Praying With Mary*
has given them profound insight into Mary's interior
life.

ISBN: 0-914544-31-4 $4.95

ATTAINING SPIRITUAL MATURITY
FOR CONTEMPLATION:
According to St. John of the Cross
Rev. Venard Poslusney, O. Carm.

Are you ready for a deeper walk in the Spirit? Are you
willing to make the effort to go the full way? Father
Venard's book will inspire and give you practical direc-
tion. It will serve as a guide to the great treasures in
the mystical writings of St. John of the Cross.

                    Rev. George De Prizio, C.S.C

ISBN: 0-914544-04-7 $2.95

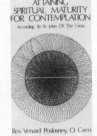

JONAH
The Spirituality of a Runaway Prophet
Rev. Roman Ginn, O.C.S.O.

With humor and clarity, Padre Ginn retells the story of Jonah, his attempted flight from God and his harsh awakening to a divine reality. While acquiring a new appreciation for this very human prophet, we come to see that Jonah's story is also our own. We are reminded that if we are to experience the freedom of mature Christianity, we must enter the darkness of the tomb with Christ, as Jonah did, so that we can rise to new life.

ISBN: 0-914544-21-7 $2.95

LINGER WITH ME:
Moments Aside with Jesus
Msgr. David E. Rosage

The author guides us on a spiritual journey to that quiet resting place within ourselves, to find peace and renewal in the love of God. Thirty-one scriptural meditations, plus an instructive outline for daily or weekly contemplation, bring the reader into a deeper union with the Holy Trinity.

ISBN: 0-914544-29-2 $4.95

DISCOVERING PATHWAYS TO PRAYER
Msgr. David E. Rosage

A simple but profound book which explains the many ways and forms of prayer by which the person hungering for closer union with God may find him.

Emmanuel Spillane, O.C.S.O
Abbot, Our Lady of the Holy Trinity Abbey
Huntsville, Utah

ISBN: 0-914544-08-X $4.95

SUFFICIENT GRACE
Elfrieda D. Drescher

How God's grace strengthened and sustained a polio victim and her family through more than 25 years of physical, mental and spiritual testing and helped them to find His Kingdom through each other. The inspiring story of one family's journey—with God's help— through years of struggle.

ISBN: 0-914544-66-7 $4.95

FINDING PEACE IN PAIN
The Reflections of a Christian Psychotherapist
Yvonne C. Hebert, M.A., M.F.C.C.

This insightful book offers a positive approach to prayer that will help us to overcome the paralyzing effects of emotional hurt from difficult life situations that can't be avoided or changed. Yvonne Hebert, a practicing psychotherapist, draws from examples involving her own clients in order to show us the way to *Finding Peace in Pain*.

ISBN: 0-914544-53-5 $3.95

DISCERNMENT
Seeking God in Every Situation
Rev. Chris Aridas

The ability to discover God's will and plan for our lives is not only possible but vitally necessary for all who seek to follow the Spirit. Fr. Aridas takes discernment out of the realm of mystery and here sets forth a clear, concise process by which we may find God and thereby discover His will.

ISBN: 0-914544-37-3 $4.95

MIDLIFE
Triumph – Not Crisis
Elizabeth Burg

Elizabeth Burg, wife and mother, rich in understanding and experience, looks at the problems and gifts of midlife from a Christian perspective. She offers practical advice concerning the attitudes and actions that can bring joy and fulfillment to these years.

ISBN: 0-914544-63-2 $4.95

MOURNING: The Healing Journey
Rev. Kenneth J. Zanca

Out of his own grief, Father Zanca has written a sensitive, sympathetic and helpful book. In this very human presentation he tells of his anger at God as well as the experiences that led eventually to peace. Father Zanca offers no pietistic resolves, but shows how a valiant struggle with grief can result in triumphant faith.

ISBN: 0-914544-30-6 $4.95

SPIRITUAL DIRECTION:
Contemporary Readings
Rev. Kevin Culligan, O.C.D.

This book was compiled especially for those entering spiritual direction, either as directors or directees. It is an excellent introduction to this exciting ministry in today's Church. The author, a licensed psychologist, has devoted many years to research, teaching, writing and practice in the field.

ISBN: 0-914544-43-8 $5.95

SOUNDINGS: A Daily Guide Through Scriptural Prayer For Today's Christian
Rev. Chris Aridas

This guidebook for reading Scripture in prayer and meditation is organized around 52 themes, with over 500 scriptural passages and commentary to facilitate personal reflection. A helpful guide for all praying Christians in their journey of faith.

ISBN: 0-914544-71-3 $4.95

COMMUNION OF SAINTS
Rev. George A. Maloney, S.J.

The dynamic love relationship of all the members of the Mystical Body, both living and dead, is a truly consoling and challenging aspect of our faith. The author examines this relationship from historical, psychological, and spiritual standpoints, and discusses its direct effect on our lives.

ISBN: 0-914544-73-X $4.95

SPEAK LORD; I HEAR
Rev. George A. Maloney, S.J.

The author, a renowned spiritual teacher and retreat master, offers us new inspiration as he addresses the universal quest for intimacy with God. The reader is guided to a more focused communion with God through the Holy Spirit.

ISBN: 0-914544-69-1 $4.95

NEW CHILDREN'S DEPARTMENT

NOAH AND THE ARK

Written and Illustrated by Jan Hughes

Take advantage of the fantastic opportunity Living Flame Press is offering you to join the exciting voyage of *Noah and the Ark*. On board you and your children will meet Noah, his wife, his sons and his sons' wives. You will also meet two of every living thing on earth. Each page is fabulously full of colorful, detailed illustrations that are guaranteed to captivate and enchant children of all ages . . . Climb aboard and journey with Noah and his family to God's promised land.

"Fabulous Color"
"Beautifully Illustrated"

ISBN: 0-914544-98-5   Softcover-$6.95
ISBN: 0-914544-97-7   Hardcover-$9.95

THE ANGEL'S QUEST
Kathy Thomas
Children, Hardcover

In this lovely, unusual story, orphaned baby Thoma is entrusted to a serene and determined angel for placement. The final choice is with a poor Christian family. They rejoice and lovingly share their simple blessings. This is an excellent original religious story; it is refreshing and inspiring without being didactic.

School Library Journal

ISBN: 0-914544-99-3 $9.95

Additional books from
LIVING FLAME PRESS
*Available at your bookstore
or call or write:*
Living Flame Press
325 Rabro Drive, Hauppauge, NY 11788
(516) 348-5251

ORDER FORM

Adventure in Spiritual Direction	$2.95		Mary: Pathway to Fruitfulness	4.95
Angel's Quest.... (hardcover)	9.95		Midlife Triumph	4.95
Attaining Spiritual Maturity	2.95		Mourning: The Healing Journey	6.95
Becoming a Christian Person	4.95		Noah and the Ark (softcover)	9.95
Born-Again Catholic	2.95		Noah and the Ark (hardcover)	5.95
Bread for the Eating	4.95		On the Palm of His Hand	2.95
Communion of Saints	2.95		Poor in Spirit	2.95
Covenant Love	5.95		Prayer of Love	2.95
Desert Harvest	2.95		Prayer: The Eastern Tradition	4.95
Desert Place	4.95		Praying With Mary	3.95
Discernment	2.95		Praying With Scripture	2.95
Discovering Pathways to Prayer	4.95		Presence Through the Word	4.95
Encountering the Lord in Daily Life	4.95		Post Charismatic Experience	2.95
Enfolded by Christ	2.95		Reasons for Rejoicing	5.95
Family Spirituality	4.95		Reconciliation	2.95
Finding Peace in Pain	3.95		Returning Sun	4.95
Finding the Mystic Within You	4.95		Revelation, Book of	2.95
Formed by His Word	2.95		Seeking Purity of Heart	4.95
Grains of Wheat	3.95		Soundings	2.95
Indwelling Presence	4.95		Source of Life	4.95
Jonah	2.95		Speak Lord; I Hear	5.95
Journey Into Contemplation	3.95		Spiritual Direction	4.95
Judas Within	2.95		Sufficient Grace	2.95
Linger With Me	4.95		Thirsting for God in Scripture	3.95
Living Here and Hereafter	2.95		Thoughts & Reflections	2.95
Loneliness is for Loving	4.95		To Comfort and Confront	2.95
Love Explosion	2.95		To Live as Jesus Did	4.95
Love in Action	5.95		Turning Road	2.95
Lubov	5.95		Union with the Lord	2.95
Manna in the Desert	5.95		Who Do You Say You Are?	4.95
			Who Is This God You Pray To?	2.95
			Wholeness	2.95
			Wisdom Instructs Her Children	3.95

PAYMENT IN ADVANCE REQUIRED FOR ALL ORDERS

WE ACCEPT *ONLY* INTERNATIONAL POSTAL MONEY ORDERS IN UNITED STATES CURRENCY AS PAYMENT FOR ORDERS FROM OUTSIDE THE UNITED STATES.

QUANTITY DISCOUNTS: Over $50.00 —10%
Over $75.00 —15%

SHIPPING AND HANDLING CHARGES:
Up to $25.00 .... 11% **($1.95 Minimum)**
$25.01 to $50.00 .... 9%
$50.01 and Up 7%

BOOKSTORES AND RETREAT HOUSES:
Trade Discounts available on orders of 5 books or more.
Payment: net 30 days

TOTAL AMOUNT ORDERED	
Discount (if applicable)	
Sub Total	
SHIPPING & HANDLING	
TAX (NYS Residents Add Local %)	
Total	

☐ Payment enclosed.

An88LA

Name _____

Address _____

City _____

State _____ Zip _____

1   2   3

Living Flame Press   325 Rabro Drive   Hauppauge, N.Y.   11788
516-348-5252